W9-AAU-315

CRUCIVERBALISM

SELECTED BOOKS BY

Stanley Newman (Author/Editor)

The Million Word Crossword Dictionary (with Daniel R. Stark)
10,000 Answers: The Ultimate Trivia Encyclopedia (with Hal Fittipaldi)
The Million Word Crossword Answer Book (with Daniel R. Stark)
Assorted Trifles: Thousands of Tantalizing Trivia Tidbits
Stanley Newman's Opus 100 Crosswords
Stanley Newman's Ultimate Trivia Crosswords
Stanley Newman's Movie Mania Crosswords
Stanley Newman's Screen Legend Crosswords
Stanley Newman's Sitcom Crosswords
Stanley Newman's Cartoon Crosswords
Stanley Newman's Comedy Legend Crosswords
Stanley Newman's What a Character! Crosswords
Stanley Newman's American Originals Crosswords
Stanley Newman's Literary Crosswords
Stan's Saturday Crosswords
Stanley Newman's Sunday Crosswords
Random House Vacation Crosswords
Random House Four Seasons Crossword Omnibus
Random House Masterpiece Crosswords
Random House Golf Crosswords
Random House Monster Sunday Crossword Omnibus
Random House Monster Crossword Omnibus
Random House Sunday Crossword Megamonster
Newsday Sunday Crossword Puzzles
Newsday Daily Crossword Puzzles

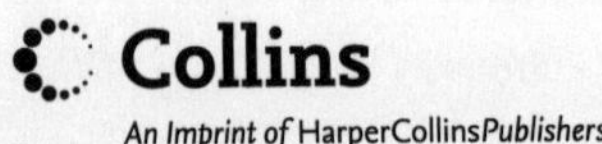
Collins
An Imprint of HarperCollinsPublishers

CRUCIVERBALISM

A Crossword Fanatic's Guide to Life in the Grid

Stanley Newman
with Mark Lasswell

 For information, address HarperCollins Publishers, 10 East 53rd Street, New York, NY 10022.

HarperCollins books may be purchased for educational, business, or sales promotional use. For information, please write: Special Markets Department, HarperCollins Publishers, 10 East 53rd Street, New York, NY 10022.

FIRST EDITION

Designed by Lorie Pagnozzi

Library of Congress Cataloging-in-Publication Data has been applied for.

ISBN-10: 0-06-089060-6

ISBN-13: 978-0-06-089060-5

06 07 08 09 10 ◆/RRD 10 9 8 7 6 5 4 3 2 1

ACKNOWLEDGMENTS

FOR THEIR HELP IN MAKING THIS BOOK POSSIBLE, I WOULD LIKE TO THANK:

—**Joseph Vallely,** my literary agent, whose idea it was

—**Toni Sciarra,** my editor at HarperCollins

—**Mark Lasswell,** my collaborator, who molded my words into sparkling prose

—and **Will Shortz,** whose singular presence in the puzzle world truly made it all possible

CONTENTS

CHAPTER ONE

Crossfire: The Pipsqueak Manifesto

I remember the date when I declared war on the *New York Times* crossword puzzle: October 19, 1984. It was the day of the LOA outrage. My annoyance with the *Times* puzzle was simmering much of that fall—who can forget the affront to *Good Times* TV star Jimmie Walker, lumped into the clue "Comedian or former N.Y. mayor" for an answer that employed the less-than-dy-no-mite! spelling, JIMMY WALKER? Then there was the infamous "parting words" clue for FAREWELL, an answer that a plurality of solvers—and lexicographers—would regard as one word. But LOA was what pushed me over the edge. Or, rather, its clue did: "Seat of Wayne County, Utah."

Now, in the course of building a crossword puzzle, it is sometimes necessary to include the sequence L-O-A when you've got an exquisite stack of words that will work only if you can keep those three letters in the mix. Fair enough. The painless tradition is to give the clue "Mauna ___," for the famous volcano in Hawaii, and move on. No doubt *Times* puzzle editor Eugene Maleska wanted to find a fresh way of cluing LOA. But "Seat of Wayne County, Utah" was beyond the pale. Aside from the 364 residents of Loa, Utah, at the time (I looked it up) and possibly a few cross-country truck drivers, it was unlikely that anyone who sat down with the *Times* puzzle that day would have known the three-letter answer to the Wayne County clue.

A small matter, you say? Ha! The LOA incident epitomized what was ailing the sickly *Times* puzzle in those days. A formerly grand institution known for its daring innovations, delightful wordplay, and all-around cerebrally stimulating fun had been reduced to this: A three-block dead zone in the puzzle, where you could get the L and O and still not be sure of the answer unless your last name was Rand or McNally. Getting it right depended entirely on answering the crossing words correctly—and spelling them right, too, since you had no way of knowing if the seat of Wayne County was correctly spelled LOA, LOB, or LOC—or LOX, LOY, or LOZ, for that matter. That was a sorry predicament, but the truly annoying thing about the clue was what it reflected about the *Times* puzzle. You didn't know what the seat of Wayne County was, you didn't care what the seat of Wayne County was once you'd learned it, and you wouldn't ever use that information again in your life unless it came up again in the *Times* puzzle. Mauna Loa, on the other hand, was a place of some renown—there was a certain value attached to it beyond its use in puzzling; you might hope to visit it one day on a vacation in Hawaii, or you might feel you'd learned something interesting if, in a well-crafted puzzle, you found out that the phrase "*mauna loa*" means "long mountain." My apologies to the people of Loa, but "Seat of Wayne County, Utah" was a useless piece of information that made it into the *Times* puzzle solely because Eugene Maleska took a pedant's pleasure in flummoxing other people with obscure facts.

When the Wayne County crime against crosswords was committed, I had been publishing a newsletter, the *Crossworder's Own Newsletter*, for less than a year. Occasionally I'd take potshots at the *Times* puzzles for mistakes, pointless trivia, and their seeming hostility toward—or outright ignorance of—the contemporary world (Maleska once rejected a puzzle because he maintained that one answer, CAR SEAT, was a "forced" concept dreamed up by the puzzler. Tell that to his kids.). But now, post-LOA, I took up the battle against the *Times* as a crusade. Resentment against Maleska's regime had been brewing for years in the puzzle community, but taking on the Bigfoot of the business directly was considered lunacy. A strange parallel world had developed in the early 1980s as the best solvers and puzzlemakers in the country began flocking to *Games* magazine, even as the *Times*—which these aficionados

had once revered—continued to reign in the public's mind as the ultimate in puzzling. It was still the most prestigious showcase for puzzlemakers.

I knew a lot of the expert puzzlers because I had taken up crosswords with a passion a few years earlier—becoming a cruciverbalist, as crossword enthusiasts sometimes like to call themselves—after having been just a casual solver in the past. But I did have a competitive streak and a good memory for the sort of facts that crop up in puzzles, and after entering a crossword contest on a whim in 1981, I was hooked. (The American Crossword Puzzle Tournament in Stamford, Connecticut, only a few years old at that point, has since become an institution among puzzlers and is still held at the Stamford Marriott each March.) I threw myself into learning how to solve puzzles faster, began building a collection of many hundreds of notecards recording unfamiliar words I encountered—yes, I was a tad obsessive about it—and in a matter of months I was winning tournaments. The quality of the puzzles at the tournaments, the fascinating people who made them and solved them, the general atmosphere of sparky intelligence and good humor at the events—all of this seemed worlds away from the dreary *Times* puzzle emanating from West 43rd Street in Manhattan seven days a week. The very people who were so lively and brilliant at the tournaments were often the same folks sending puzzles they'd constructed to Maleska and crossing their fingers in the hope that they hadn't violated any of his myriad strictures, thus inviting another one of his infamously vicious rejection letters.

This was an era when typical clues at the *Times* would refer to a "Famed soprano" or "First words of St. John's Gospel, Latin" (Answer: IN PRINCIPIO ERAT). Fun, eh? Meanwhile, in what amounted to an underground movement, crossword tournaments were beginning to take off. The American Crossword Puzzle Tournament was already fairly well established after a few years in existence, and in 1982 *Games* magazine organized the first U.S. Open Crossword Puzzle Championship. My crossword self-improvement campaign was in full force at that point, and I was intent on winning the U.S. Open a few months after having taken the American Crossword title.

Two hundred and fifty contestants made it through the mail-in phase of the U.S. Open tourney to the final competition, held at New York University. It was a feast of fascinating words and ingenious clues. Some words were unfamiliar to me but I muddled my way through to spelling them correctly; other words were ones that, I was pleased to see, I'd recently scribbled down on my note cards (KACHINA, a Hopi Indian doll, and ARUM, the name of the plant family that the jack-in-the-pulpit belongs to. It's also the name of the boxing promoter, first name Bob, but never mind). The un*Times*ian cluing was a pure delight. I was stumped for a long time—okay, probably a matter of seconds, but that's an eternity at these affairs—by the clue "Chromosome choices." Do chromosomes even *make* choices? And how could the answer fit into a four-letter space, especially when the fourth letter is probably an S, since clues given in the plural almost always generate an answer that ends in S? As I discovered, after some hasty crosswise solving that gave me a couple of letters, the inspired answer was X OR Y. I got that one right, but muffed another: In response to the clue "Arctic assistant," I wrote ELK, thinking of Santa and Rudolph. The K crossed with the first box of the answer to "Radio tuning abbreviation," but I just couldn't tune in the solution, which was FREQ for "frequency"—and would have turned the ELK into an ELF. Argh!

Despite my trans-species mistake, other competitors made even more errors, and I won the tournament. I was now completely intoxicated with crossword puzzles, but I noticed that having taught myself how to master the *solving* of puzzles, I was becoming increasingly fascinated by the constructors I was meeting at tournaments. Winning the national championship was a wonderful vindication of all the hours I'd spent teaching myself to become a better solver, but joining the top competitors in crossword puzzling didn't mean I'd reached the true elite. The editors and constructors were where the action was. It's one thing to be able to decipher a devilishly tricky clue, but it's another to dream it up. The constructors at the U.S. Open were a fascinating lot. The hilarious pop-culture maven Merl Reagle constructed the championship puzzle, but the most truly memorable puzzle of the tournament came from Henry Hook, who's the closest thing to an avant-garde artist in the crossword world. His offering was entitled "Sound Thinking," with many of the clues announced over a loudspeaker. It was an audacious (audio-acious?), totally amusing idea. Amusing, and unnerving, because the contestants had to fret over how to handle this distracting last-minute curveball—after all, save for all the sighs and groans, solving a crossword puzzle is supposed to be a silent pursuit.

The more I talked to these puzzle-constructing folks, the more I realized that they shared my frustration with the *Times.* With *Games* magazine as their primary vehicle, they were putting out puzzles marked by a shared interest in clever clues, a contempt for "crosswordese" (those tiresomely obscure words that seem to exist solely for the convenience of puzzle constructors), and an assumption that Americans in the second half of the 20th century were likely to be better versed in the minutiae of pop culture than of the Hapsburg Dynasty. It was exhilarating working on their puzzles; some of the crosswords were so diabolically inventive that you felt flattered that the constructor thought you were up to solving them.

In other words, these constructors were the anti-Maleskas. And yet, for all their wild, palpable love for words and wordplay, they were curiously circumspect about publicly criticizing the Maleska regime running the puzzle that was supposed to be the gold standard of the business. The puzzle in the Sunday *Times* magazine was by then a cultural touchstone; in a public place on a Sunday almost anywhere in the U.S., you were almost certain to see someone working on it. The *Times*' daily and weekend puzzles were widely syndicated and widely emulated, which meant that the paper held enormous sway over the way crossword devotees did puzzles and over the way newcomers perceived what crosswords were all about. The paper also held the purse strings for constructors—to the extent that an endeavor that pays as badly as constructing crossword puzzles could be said to warrant a purse. More like a coin purse. In those days, the *Times* paid about $35 for a daily puzzle. But it wasn't about making a living by constructing puzzles; almost everyone in the business had a full-time job (I was a Wall Street bond analyst at the time). No, having your puzzle published in the *Times* was simply an emblem of having reached the top of the puzzle business. Or at least that had been the case for a few decades, and people were unlikely to abandon that belief simply because in 1977 the *Times* puzzle had been taken over by Eugene Maleska.

Maleska, I was not surprised to learn, was a former Latin teacher and Bronx school superintendent. His pedantic background was on display every day in the *New York Times*, where you were expected not only to be intimately familiar with the opera world, but also to know that the answer for "Dwarf buffalo" is ANOA. (What's the difference between this one and Merl Reagle's KACHINA? I'm actually kind of glad to know about the Hopi doll, and expect that Merl is, too. I seriously doubt that even Maleska cared about alternative names for the dwarf buffalo; ANOA is one of those words you see in crossword puzzles because the constructor needed that vowel-heavy sequence of letters and was happy to discover it actually formed a word, any word, no matter how obscure.) Even though Maleska had constructed puzzles for the *Times* for years and was known for having come up with entertaining innovations like the step-quote puzzle that unfolds in layers across a grid, he seemed to have taken the title of puzzle editor as a grave responsibility. His predecessor, Will Weng, was the *Times*' crossword editor from 1969 to 1977, and puzzles on his watch reflected the rules-challenging spirit of the era. He encouraged unusual ideas for puzzle themes, including theme answers that were palindromes, for instance, or that chronically missed a vowel. Merl Reagle remembers him allowing a clue, "Optometrist's cherished alma mater," that required the answer EYE LOVE U—a solution not based in any reality other than the sheer fun of the pun.

When Maleska took over, it was as if he had vowed to put an end to all this frivolity. He would have flunked EYE LOVE U as a forced answer. He seemed to relish humiliating anyone who attempted to take a fresh approach to building puzzles; he gave every indication that he regarded the *Times* puzzle's natural audience as the residents of a retirement home for university dons.

I thought the situation was intolerable. In religion, they say, there's no zealot like the convert. The same must be true of crossword puzzlers. I was a convert. A lot of the constructors and competitors I met at the tournaments had become infatuated with crossword puzzles as teenagers or even earlier, but I was a newcomer to the scene. I was flabbergasted that a pastime with so much fun and intellectual stimulation to offer could be reduced, in its most public showcase, to such an uninspired form of rote work. Many in the puzzle world seemed resigned to waiting Maleska out in the hope that this benighted era would pass. I didn't see any point in waiting. Then came the Wayne County/LOA atrocity. I decided then to start my crusade against the *Times.* I certainly wasn't going to change Maleska's hidebound way of thinking, and there wasn't much chance of convincing his newspaper bosses to reassign him to, oh, the obituary department. But at the very least I wanted to get the word out to the average puzzle solver: There was a new generation of puzzle constructors on the scene who shared a lot of the same ideas about fresh approaches to crosswords, but whose sensibility you'd never find reflected in what amounted to the country's crossword puzzle of record.

I felt a kind of urgency about the matter, not least because at the very time when the country's most visible crossword puzzle seemed to be getting stodgier and less appealing, there was an eruption of public interest in pastimes that involved mental challenges.

Millions of folks were playing a new game called Trivial Pursuit, and the TV quiz show *Jeopardy!* had become hugely popular. These games had uncovered a massive public appetite for brainteasers that tested both general knowledge and familiarity with popular culture. Crossword puzzles were missing an opportunity to bring in a new generation of fans as well as hold on to solvers who might be getting bored with newspaper crossword puzzles across the country that, thanks to the *Times* effect, were almost uniformly tedious.

So I ramped up the criticism of the *Times* in the *Newsletter.* Sometimes I used Maleska's own book about crossword puzzling, *Across and Down*, as a cudgel against him. In the book, he very sensibly prescribed: "When an Across word is abstruse, the pro makes sure that its vertical crossers are all easy words with relatively simple clues." Exactly right. Figure out where the abstruseness and easiness are in these intersections taken from *Times* puzzles in December 1984:

- "Commune in Tuscany" (PRATO) crossing "Island at head of Baffin Bay" (DEVON)
- "Spiny acacias" (BABULS) crossing "Philippine native" (BATAN)

Hmmm, I wonder how you could come up with clues that might actually make these examples conform to the rule that Maleska stated in his own book. DEVON is a rather well-known place in

England, so the Baffin Bay reference is unnecessarily "abstruse." And BATAN could be deftly clued with "_____ eyelash."

It wasn't just the useless obscurity of the *Times* puzzles that irritated me. Despite all the pretense of erudition and unforgiving exactitude they seemed to promote, the puzzles were often defective on the most basic levels. The same puzzles that might demand you know "The lower Rhine arm" is the WAAL (what was it with the atlas obsession back then?) could fail even to keep their own conceits working properly. Thus, you had a puzzle with an amusing theme that would give clues with paired first names of famous people asking for answers with the corresponding last names that, taken together, formed another word. That's a fine approach, and it's entertaining to see "Dyan/Lucille" form CANNONBALL, and "Paul/Ayn" make KRUGERRAND. But what to make of "Greco/Clara"? The answer the *Times* wanted was ELBOW, but that corrupts the "First name"/LAST NAME symmetry of the theme: The format would have demanded the clue "El/Clara" and produced the nonsensical answer GRECOBOW. (If you want to get really persnickety about it—and a maniacal persnicketyness is the essence of crossword puzzling—the clue is also damaged goods because "El Greco" was just the artist's nickname. He was born Domenicos Theotocopoulos. "Domenicos/Clara" and THEOTOCOPOULOSBOW, anyone?) The mistake may have originated with the constructor, but it's the editor's job to polish puzzles and avoid precisely this sort of gaffe. Maleska was famous for banning constructors for their errors.

When I started regularly pointing out the *Times'* mistakes and preposterous word choices in my *Crossworder's Own Newsletter*—I even introduced a section called the "Keeping Up with the *Times* Department"—readers were ecstatic. It was as if they'd been suffering in silence for years, so intimidated by the pretensions of a puzzle demanding a thorough familiarity with the suburban neighborhoods of Buenos Aires that they didn't dare point out basic mistakes like the crooked ELBOW clue. I got letters and phone calls every month, as soon as people saw my latest darts aimed at the *Times*. (I also got letters pointing out my own puzzle mistakes.) Friends came up to me at tournaments, both gleeful over my guerrilla campaign, but also slightly concerned, as if we were all living in Havana and I'd been overheard in a coffee shop criticizing Castro. Was it really healthy for me, they seemed to wonder; wasn't I burning my bridges with the *Times*? Well, I didn't have a bridge to burn because I was working on Wall Street and had no crossword aspirations beyond putting out my little newsletter and competing in tournaments.

Though the *Newsletter* made a habit of tweaking the *New York Times*, I tried to be an equal-opportunity critic. The Los Angeles Times Syndicate was publishing some atrocious puzzles in the 1980s, so I happily pointed it out when they'd commit a howler like issuing a puzzle with a theme that called for celebrities' last names that are also cities (JOHN DENVER, JULIE LONDON) but boneheadedly included a country (JILL IRELAND). This from a paper that counted Hollywood in its distribution area. But the influence of the *New York Times* was such that, if you were going to be a bomb-thrower on behalf of what was increasingly being called "new wave" puzzles, then Maleska's East Coast fortress had to be the primary target. Plus, it was just so much fun to tug on Superman's cape. Maleska's own writing on crosswords provided an endless supply of ammunition to use against him. "Amateurish creations abound in the puzzle world," he once wrote, pointing out that such laughable work contains "a plethora of esoterica and crosswordese." I'd happily quote lines like this in the *Newsletter* and then point out that a single *Times* puzzle called for answers including BLE, CERE, EMIR, ESNES, ILEAC, LAC, LEROS, LEV, NAPPES, ORALE, RETE, SMEE, STELAR, STOMA, TOPIS, and UPE. (Don't have any idea what most of these mean? Be grateful, be very grateful.)

I don't know at what point Maleska decided I was the enemy. Maybe it was when I started trying to get him fired. In 1987, Max Frankel took over from Abe Rosenthal as Executive Editor of the *Times*, and I published Frankel's address at the paper in the *Newsletter*, urging readers to "take action" and tell Maleska's new boss how terrible his puzzles were. Or maybe it was when newspaper reporters started writing about the conflict between new-wave puzzlers and the old guard, citing me as the chief instigator. The *Orlando Sentinel* ran a story in March 1988 that included photos of me and Maleska, with mine on top, which must have infuriated him (this was a guy who went public in 1988 with his outrage over not being pictured along with such genuine editorial titans of the business as former *Times* puzzle editors Margaret Farrar and Will Weng in *Games* magazine's commemorative issue for the 75th birthday of the crossword puzzle). The *Sentinel* piece ended with the news that Maleska had sent a note to his bosses saying that, though he had no intention of retiring, he did have a few recommendations about who should succeed him. "I can tell you this," he told the reporter. "It won't be Stanley Newman."

Much of the war between the new wave and Maleska was fought in newspaper and magazine articles in the late 1980s, with headlines that inevitably used the phrase "Cross Words." Maleska really went after me in an article about the conflict in the New York City weekly *7 Days,* his disdain practically dripping off the page. He dismissed the new wave as "the Newman ripple." And he claimed—astonishingly—that I had originally tried to recruit him as co-editor of my newsletter, and then he quoted his response to the idea of working with me: "Who, that pipsqueak?"

Pipsqueak! Oh, it was wonderful. The *7 Days* article had many priceless nuggets—such as the fact that when a solver wrote to Maleska complaining that he had included the derogative term

WETBACK in a puzzle, the editor replied with a letter denying any racist intent, loftily adding, "My poems and articles on brotherhood have been widely acclaimed." The article also reported—accurately—that I had once made a peace offering to Maleska, suggesting that we meet over dinner to discuss our differences (the Crossword Hall of Fame was being drawn up at the time, and it seemed appropriate to make nice). But he rejected my overture. And now he was calling me the p-word.

Even as Maleska remained embedded at the *Times*, the new wave was clearly making inroads elsewhere in the country. Merl Reagle was hired to create the Sunday puzzle of the *San Francisco Examiner.* The same month that the *Orlando Sentinel* story ran, I was hired by *Newsday* to edit their Sunday puzzle. The job couldn't have come at a better time. I'd lost my Wall Street position a few months earlier in the 1987 crash, and had decided to try to make a living solely from crossword puzzles as a creator, editor, and syndicator. It was in 1987 that I published in the *Newsletter* what amounted to my manifesto. Bear with me while I quote a few major points:

"Crosswords should be fun, they should be challenging, and they should be enjoyed by any reasonably literate person."

"Crosswordese and obscure words are prohibited (only occasional exceptions are made for otherwise outstanding work)."

"Clues must be balanced in general knowledge (no more than one non-theme reference to football or opera in a puzzle)."

"The most serious problem facing the crossword world today is that it's being left behind by the public-at-large in the trivia/game show resurgence of recent years . . . We believe the reason for this is that the average person's exposure to crosswords comes from the daily newspaper, and not one weekday newspaper crossword in this country comes even close to adhering to the standards listed above."

"We have a plan for changing this state of affairs. It involves making more people aware of the existence of 'solver-friendly' contemporary crosswords; having more solvers demand higher standards from their puzzle editors; and, the pinnacle of our plan, getting contemporary puzzles into a major weekday newspaper."

In the end, the new wave made an end run around Eugene Maleska. The *Times* never did fire him. He passed away in 1993. By then, though, the beginning of the end of the war was already in sight. In 1992, I was delighted to become the first editor of a daily new-wave puzzle, at *Newsday.* When it was time for *Times* editors to reach outside the bunker to find a new puzzle chief, they discovered that the terrain of the crossword world was being transformed. Anyone under the age of 60 whom they might have approached with the job was likely to be a card-carrying member of the new wave, so the selection of an editor with a more contemporary outlook was almost inevitable. But the *Times*, having tolerated such an intolerable situation with the puzzle for so long,

surprised everyone by making the best possible choice in hiring Will Shortz, who'd done heroic work at *Games* magazine promoting the crossword revolution. Once Shortz was installed, the war that had lasted well over a decade was truly over. It had been a battle fueled by a wonderful mix of fun and the self-righteousness that comes with fighting the establishment, but now we were the establishment. To the rebellious spirit, we had to bid farewell. And that's FAREWELL—one word, thank you.

CHAPTER TWO

A Day in the Life of a Crossword Fanatic

Computers: blessing or scourge? A decade ago. crossword puzzle constructors were like a medieval guild, fashioning their handicrafts as they had been made for generations, with pencil and paper and reference books. The sheer pain-in-the-neck aspect of putting together a salable puzzle kept most of the bluffers out of the game. But with the advent of crossword-making software, any fool could become a constructor with a click of a mouse—and many did. The trouble is that computer software might efficiently riffle through the entire dictionary and produce the answers required to fill any grid you could throw at it. But the puzzles generated by software are too often stuffed with junk: foreign phrases, weird abbreviations, and obscure words so unfamiliar they don't even qualify as crosswordese.

It's not that I represent some sort of Amish wing of the puzzle-constructing trade, scraping away with pencil and paper, muttering about the curse of modern technology. In fact, I use crossword software. But before I started using it, I had learned how to make crosswords competently. Now, I'm able to work with the raw material that the software churns out and shape it into a puzzle that I could have created with pencil and paper—only with a much smaller investment of time. What makes me cranky are the puzzles I receive that are clearly hot off the hard drive, with nary a glance from the "constructor," who more likely is just some guy who spent $49.95 on the software, figuring that if he can start selling puzzles for $50 apiece, he'll have made a profitable little investment indeed.

Long may these worms operate in the red. They're an insult to puzzledom. Luckily for me, the most obvious target for these mouse-wielding entrepreneurs is the *New York Times*, where Will Shortz spends a significant part of his day politely batting them away. At *Newsday*, I happily rely on a handful of regular contributors, with an occasional new constructor entering the mix. When a software-generated puzzle does come in from someone who spent more effort addressing the envelope or typing in the e-mail address than making the puzzle, it rankles because the carelessness touches a raw nerve: Crosswords struggle hard enough for respect outside the puzzle world without having to contend with slights from the would-be constructors themselves.

The backhanded treatment of crosswords in the very newspapers that publish them has been an irksome tendency since the puzzles began appearing more than 90 years ago. I can't count the number of times in the past dozen years I've seen comics take swipes at crosswords as ridiculous exercises in trivia and obscure words. It's as if the new-wave revolution in puzzling never happened—even though the evidence is often just a few column inches away from the smug comic making the easy joke. But I'll grant that comic-strip artists can take whatever license they like with their out-of-date potshots. No doubt they stem from the rivalrous feelings engendered by the belief—shared equally by comic-strip makers and crossword editors—that *our* patch of real estate in the newspaper is the main reason why most people buy the thing in the first place. (As any newspaper editor knows, if you change White House correspondents, you'll never hear a peep from readers, but if you alter the crossword or change the comics page, take the phone off the hook because it's not going to stop ringing for a couple of weeks—or until the old reader favorite is restored.)

My bigger beef is with newspapers' historically cavalier treatment of crosswords, particularly the papers' frequent refusal even to attach bylines to them. As for noting the editor's name? Forget it. An e-mail address? Are you kidding? Each crossword constructor brings a particular vocabulary, sense of humor, pop-culture taste, and historical orientation to the puzzles he or she constructs. Just like any news article or opinion column, puzzles are the idiosyncratic expression of one person's sensibility—or, rather, two people's: the constructor's and the interfering puzzle editor's—yet many newspapers simply

refuse to run puzzle bylines, treating the crosswords as if they were products stamped out on a factory line.

But more about that later. Happily, my editors at *Newsday* don't fall into any of these categories. They agree with my position on bylines, I'm pleased to report, which reflects a generally puzzle-friendly atmosphere at the paper. In fact, John Mancini, who was named editor in 2004, is a crossword fan, marking the first time in my nearly two decades of association with *Newsday* that the person in charge is an active crossword fan. This is a mixed blessing: It's nice to know that the boss appreciates a good crossword puzzle, but it also means I jolly well better stay on my toes. If a newspaper editor is a big football fan and closely reads everything in the paper on the subject, he's not going to be happy when he stumbles over a mistake in a football story. When he's a crossword fan, the puzzle editor has an unsettling piece of knowledge hanging over his head: *A goof in the Sunday puzzle could ruin the boss's entire weekend.* Not that this has ever happened, or that Mr. Mancini would be anything but civilized and understanding and magnificent if it did. But still.

The puzzle-positive tenor at *Newsday* means that most of my waking moments are devoted to the pleasant business of making my own crosswords, tweaking those of my contributors, shepherding puzzles through the publishing process and generally attending to my puzzle business. My life in the grid hasn't always been so idyllic. It didn't even really begin until I was almost 30. Nowadays I'm fortunate enough to be one of a handful of people who can make a living in the crossword business. That fact, plus my history of winning tournaments and setting fastest-solving records, prompts the quite understandable assumption among crossword puzzle fans that I must have grown up as some sort of prodigy, clearing away the Rice Krispies on my high-chair tray so I could do the Sunday *New York Times* puzzle in crayon. That was not at all the case. My mother does recall my working on the *TV Guide* crossword puzzle as a child in Brooklyn, but the fact that I was reading *TV Guide* in elementary school is the more telling point: I have always been fascinated by facts about television and movies, sports and history—an interest that became extremely useful when, as an adult, I came to appreciate the exquisite way that crossword puzzles weave together a love of language, wordplay, and factual knowledge. But all through my years at Stuyvesant High School and Brooklyn College, doing crosswords was hardly more than a minor form of recreation. My parents didn't even subscribe to the *New York Times*; as a teenager, I would sometimes pick up the *Times*' Sunday magazine at my grandparents' house and sit on their porch, trying to solve it. I considered it a big deal if I could fill in just one section of the puzzle.

In my 20s, I started regularly working on the *Times* crossword during the subway ride to my job in Manhattan doing market research,

but it was just a way to pass the time. I was no more and no less interested in crossword puzzles than I was in playing Monopoly or Scrabble. But I do have a competitive streak, especially concerning cerebral topics, so when I heard about a Scrabble tournament in Brooklyn in the mid-1970s, I decided on a whim to sign up. I thought I played Scrabble pretty well, and I knew enough obscure words to annoy friends when we played, so I thought it might be fun to try my skills against strangers.

"Humbling" doesn't describe the experience of playing against the fanatics who showed up. "Abject humiliation" comes closer, but doesn't quite capture the quality of sheer fright at seeing human brains operating on a level with which I was unfamiliar. I felt like everybody else was playing with Scrabble tiles while I was fumbling with kindergarten blocks.

The Scrabble debacle—Scrabbacle?—should have cured me of any impulse to join word-related competitions. But a few years later, I saw an advertisement on the crossword-puzzle page of the *Times* announcing the second annual American Crossword Puzzle Tournament in Stamford, Connecticut, and I was intrigued. My experience in the Scrabble tournament had demonstrated to me that my knowledge of the obscure words that constitute Scrabblese was too thin to make me competitive with hardcore players (if you see the letters "TWA" and think "airline" instead of "a Scottish variant of the word 'two,' worth six points unless you can work the 'w' onto a triple-letter square in which case it's worth 14 points," then I'd recommend avoiding Scrabble tournaments). My mind was overstuffed with trivia, as were the Scrabble power players', but while they were lexiconical monomaniacs, focused solely on rearranging letters to make words, I was a Renaissance man of almost completely useless information. I could tell you—and I'm not necessarily proud of this—not only that Trans World Airlines was named Transcontinental and Western Air when Howard Hughes bought it, but also that Hughes' first wife was Texas socialite Ella Rice, who was long gone by the time Hughes was supposedly inventing the push-up bra for Jane Russell to wear in the 1943 Western he was directing entitled *The Outlaw* (I could go on, but what's the point, unless it's in the service of solving a crossword clue?). Although I couldn't compete with Scrabblers in their pure knowledge of how to hammer a random slew of letters into an actual, legitimate, you-could-look-it-up word, no matter how otiose—er, useless—it might be, I was fascinated by words themselves, especially by their tricky shades of meaning.

I suspected that these traits might reduce the likelihood of my humiliation in a crossword puzzle tournament, and I was certainly interested in finding a happier memory of competing to supplant the one of the Brooklyn massacre. Still, it took me two years to screw up the courage to enter the American Crossword Puzzle Tournament after first seeing the ad in 1979.

The people you see in hotel lobbies are almost by definition idling, whether they're killing time by staring vacantly at the bland décor or watching for someone they're supposed to meet up with. That wasn't the case at the Stamford Marriott when I arrived for the weekend tournament; even the idlers in the lobby were furiously working on crossword puzzles, like fighters shadow-boxing in the locker room before heading into the ring. The tournament had 125 entrants, which sounds like a lot, until you consider that we were competing in a ballroom designed to hold 500. A section had been partitioned off so it didn't look like a badly attended community board meeting. It helped that, in addition to friends and family, some print and TV reporters had showed up. Yes, a crossword tournament was newsworthy. Remember, in March 1981 the phenomenon of people matching wits in person and in public just wasn't that common. *Jeopardy!* and a few other TV game shows tested contestants' (and viewers') knowledge and thinking skills, but grappling mano a mano (or frontal lobe a frontal lobe) seemed novel. It wouldn't be until a few months later, in the fall of 1981, that a couple of guys up in Canada decided to trademark the name of a new game they'd come up with. They called it Trivial Pursuit.

This was the fourth year of the Stamford tournament, and it was readily apparent who were the veterans and who, like me, were the rookies. We were the ones who entered the hotel ballroom tentatively and slightly confused-looking, as if we'd gotten lost searching for the ice machine. The veteran solvers *were* ice machines, as became evident with the first round of puzzles. Solving speed was essential, and the experienced hands used vital little streamlining tricks, like entering their answers in lowercase letters instead of the infinitesimally more time-consuming capitals. They also had an encyclopedic knowledge of crosswordese—the specialized vocabulary of words having six letters or fewer that constructors employ as building blocks for more interesting words. Crossword enthusiasts and experts on medieval history are about the only people left on earth who could readily tell you that ESNE is the answer for the clue "Anglo-Saxon laborer" (it's also the acronym of the Esperanto Society of New England).

I was startled by the dazzling speed displayed by several people seated near me at the tables set up cafeteria-style in the ballroom. But instead of feeling the helplessness I'd experienced among the Scrabblers, I was pleased to find that I was also moving quickly through the puzzles. In fact, many of the answers came to me immediately—but in my haste to keep up with the competition, I sacrificed accuracy, knocking points off my score with simple spelling mistakes.

After six puzzles on Saturday, one on Sunday morning, and then a championship round for the three top scorers, the final results were posted. I was pleased, and more than a little relieved, to find that I'd finished in 13th place. It was certainly better than my Scrabble

performance in Brooklyn. But I sensed that I could do much better if I practiced in a concerted way, not just by doing more and more crossword puzzles, but by actively trying to improve specific skills. At the Stamford Marriott, I had heard about another crossword puzzle contest being held the following month at the now-defunct Grossinger's resort hotel in the Catskills. I resolved that for the next few weeks, I'd spend evenings and lunch breaks from my Wall Street job trying to improve my solving skills. I used a stopwatch to time myself, hoping to pare off seconds as I worked on puzzles of various difficulty levels.

In the past, if a clue called for an answer that I didn't know, but that I had solved correctly by using the letters from crossing words, I just murmured thanks and moved on; now I stopped and looked up the word in the dictionary, so I'd know what it meant, I'd fix its spelling in my mind, and I'd be familiar with any secondary meaning. This last was essential, because constructors love nothing better than misdirection. The clue "Scout leader" initially conjures images of camping trips and merit badges—until you're solving the puzzle and discover that the five-letter answer ends perplexingly with the letter O. That prompts a quick rethinking of the clue: What other kind of "Scout," associated with an O-ending word, might we be talking about here? A-ha! Scout was also the name of the horse ridden by the Lone Ranger's trusted sidekick, TONTO. I taught myself to be suspicious of every word in a clue (does "kid" refer to a child or a joke or a goat?), second-guessing even the pronunciation: "Nice guy" might seem innocuous enough, except it could be pronounced "*neece* guy" by a constructor who's looking for the answer HOMME. I also tried to attack the puzzles with a new state of mind: I would focus intensely and completely on each answer as I wrote it down, even if that meant sacrificing a millisecond for each entry. In Stamford, sloppy mistakes had crept in when I started thinking about the next clue before I finished jotting down an answer.

At Grossinger's, about 50 people entered the crossword contest, many of whom I recognized from Stamford. Among them was Miriam Raphael, who was a sort of rock star of the crossword world at that point. Miriam—known to one and all as Mimi—had placed second the year before at the Marriott tournament and she had won it in 1979. Mimi has the charming quality of being mild-mannered yet gregarious. You might not be shocked to learn that many people who excel at solving crossword puzzles fall into the "loner" category—but not Mimi. I have a soft spot for her because she went out of her way to be helpful and encouraging to me from the moment I began competing in tournaments—even though, as I later learned, I had caused a bit of consternation among the puzzlers when I showed up at Stamford and displayed little appreciation for the niceties of tournament etiquette. When you've finished a puzzle, for instance, you're supposed to quietly raise your hand,

without disturbing the concentration of your fellow solvers, so that the judges can note the time. Either I failed to notice this technique, or I thought there was just an epidemic in shyness in the room, but when I finished my puzzles, I found myself madly waving them in the air like I'd found a winning lottery ticket. I was ecstatic about finishing the puzzles, and I certainly didn't want to lose precious seconds if the judges happened not to notice a more discreet signal. What can I say? I grew up in Brooklyn, and working on Wall Street hadn't exactly polished my manners.

At any rate, Mimi didn't seem to hold my gaucheness against me, and she greeted me warmly at Grossinger's. Of course, she could afford to be magnanimous—she blew away the field and won the tournament. But I was delighted to find out that I had finished fifth; I came away feeling that my preparation in the previous few weeks had paid off. I made fewer errors, and several words that I'd just committed to memory had been in the puzzles. Having those words readily in mind was a twofer: Instead of slowing me down by requiring me to build them from letters used in other words, they would now speed up solving the words around them. I was excited, because I'd been able to make a substantial improvement just by working diligently over the course of a few weeks. Now I had ten months to practice before the next tournament in Stamford.

I was a number-cruncher by day and word-cruncher at night. My wife, Marlene, might have been a little perplexed by my intensive preparation. I wasn't out in the garage tinkering with an invention that could change the world and make us rich; I was just trying to get better at doing crossword puzzles. As it turned out a few years later, this would indeed result in some financial benefit when crosswords enabled me to start a second career. But my family was understanding when I closed myself off in a room for an hour or two every night. I ramped up the techniques I had developed in preparation for the Grossinger's tournament. I bought armloads of puzzle books, solving as many crosswords as I could during the day, at lunch, or on the subway. I kept using a stopwatch to monitor my speed, but also just to get used to trying to think clearly with the tick-tick-tick pressure breathing down my neck.

At night, I pored over my puzzle solutions, comparing them with the correct answers in order to identify any lurking misspellings and to solve clues that had stumped me. I still used a dictionary to look up any unfamiliar words, but I also began writing down the words and their definitions on index cards as a way of reinforcing them in my mind. When I encountered words that I thought I knew, but that were employed with obscure secondary meanings, I wrote them down, too. Most of this work occurred as I was comparing my answers with the official solution, rather than in the course of completing the puzzle. I'd circle any incorrect squares, and circle any unfamiliar words in the grids or the clues, then go to the reference books, whether that meant riffling through the dictionary for the meanings of EXEDRA (a curved outdoor bench with a high back, or semicircular portico with seats in ancient Greece or Rome where discussions were held), or hitting the encyclopedia for details about the signers of the Declaration of Independence, or consulting an atlas for tributaries of the Seine.

As my alphabetized collection of index cards grew to nearly 2,000 entries, so did my confidence. By mid-winter, I was moving easily through most puzzles, hitting fewer and fewer speed bumps. A month before the American Crossword Puzzle Tournament, Grossinger's hosted another puzzle weekend. It was my first chance to see if all the preparation had appreciably improved my skill at competing in a tournament setting. I was glad to see that Mimi was on hand again. I knew I'd need to be able to keep up with her if I had a chance of doing well in Stamford. As we completed four puzzles in succession, I was stunned to find that I finished each puzzle a few seconds before she did. It turned out that we had both completed the puzzles without mistakes, so my slight speed advantage made me the tournament winner. It was an absolutely, deliciously thrilling moment. Here was concrete evidence that my months of training had paid off. Plus, the first-place prize was a free weekend (for two, significantly, to my wife's delight) at Grossinger's. Maybe it wasn't a Super Bowl share, but it was at least a small indication that moving up in the crossword world might have a bigger payoff than a pile of quickly solved grids.

I don't want to overstate the case, but my success at Grossinger's really was a major moment in my adult life, for this reason: Once most of us get out of high school and college, we too easily slip into thinking that our mental abilities are pretty well fixed. Oh, you might acquire new skills on various jobs over the course of your life, and you might pick up odds and ends of additional learning about history and language from television or books or magazines, but the general assumption is that the capacities we've developed in school are the intellectual cards we're dealt and the ones we'll be playing for the rest of our lives. If anything, it seems, our vocabulary atrophies over time, and all those historic dates and places that were branded on our brains the night before the 12th-grade history final gradually fade away. There was something hugely satisfying, then, about finding out that, with a little diligence and direction, I had been able not only to vastly expand my vocabulary and build a mental store of facts that I was able to tap readily, but also to make myself a better *thinker.* I saw nuances in language I'd never appreciated before, I savored witticisms that I might not have even understood in the past, and I became adept at considering information from a multitude of angles, identifying possibilities and patterns with an ease that I'd never previously sensed in myself. It was exciting, because this meant that anyone could learn these skills, that everyone has the potential to sharpen his or her mind without needing to take out a student loan and go back to college. Plus, it

was just plain fun sprinting through crossword puzzles that a year earlier I would have found daunting.

Or at least it felt like sprinting. The truth was that I actually found myself writing more slowly as I tried to be thorough and accurate, but my overall speed improved as the solutions seemed to come to me in a steady flow. That was the case in Stamford on my second visit to the American Crossword Puzzle Tournament. To my amazement, I found myself finishing puzzles faster than some of the top finishers from the previous year, and with fewer mistakes than I'd made last time around. Still, I was astonished on Sunday when the tournament organizers announced that I had made it to the Final Three.

In the championship round, only accuracy counted—speed would be considered solely as a tiebreaker. Philip Cohen, a formidable wordsmith who had won the previous year, finished the championship puzzle just before I did, and I assumed that if he'd breezed so easily through it, then he must have had 100 percent accuracy. Even though I thought it was a minor miracle that I'd even made the tournament finals, once I was there, I wanted to win. I was dejected, and assumed that everyone in the room knew Philip had won, since overhead projectors were being used so the audience could follow our solving. Then came the announcement: I had won. Philip had missed two squares, and my solution was error-free. After focusing my mind so intensely on written words for the whole weekend, I stood there in a daze as my fellow solvers clustered around to shake my hand, cameras started flashing as newspaper photographers rushed over, and reporters blurted out questions (good thing you don't get penalized for sloppy answers in interviews). It was disorienting, but not unpleasant, to go from the simmering panic of trying to untangle a knotty clue to being asked by a writer for *People* magazine if I had any pets.

The Stamford competition's billing as the "American" crossword tournament made it seem like a national competition, and indeed contestants came from all over, but the Eastern Seaboard was heavily represented among the 132 entrants in 1982. Plus, qualifying for the tournament consisted of having the inclination to spend a weekend at a Marriott in Connecticut. There was a much bigger, genuinely national beast lurking on the crossword horizon that year: the first U.S. Open Crossword Puzzle Championship, organized by *Games* magazine and directed (as were the Grossinger's and Stamford tournaments) by a certain Mr. Will Shortz. The first round would be conducted by mail, which opened the contest to anyone who could afford the cost of a stamp (20 cents for first class in 1982—ah, those were the days). *Ten thousand* people entered the U.S. Open. The media coverage of the finals in New York was even more intense than at Stamford. I won this tournament, too. I had come out of Stamford feeling confident about my abilities, but at the elite level in crosswords at that time, first-place finishes changed hands frequently—no one had won Stamford more than once. I was as stunned as anyone else that I had managed to win the Stamford and U.S. Open tournaments back to back. Having done so, I realized that I had accomplished about as much as I could hope to in the competition realm. As I mentioned in Chapter One, it was at the U.S. Open finals where I became intrigued by puzzle *constructing*, and realized that genius practitioners like Henry Hook, Merl Reagle, and Mike Shenk were probably having even more fun at the tournament than the competitors. I decided to try my hand at constructing a puzzle—how hard could it be? No doubt I would not be operating at the dizzying heights occupied by Henry & Co., but I figured that, as a now bona fide master solver, I could do a respectable job. I would quickly learn that the difference between solving puzzles and constructing them is like the difference between playing the piano and composing a symphony.

When you present the first puzzle you've ever constructed to the members of your bowling team and they scan the contents briefly before giving you a pitying look, you know you've got a few things to learn about puzzle-building. Despite my frustrations with the pedantry of the Maleskacized *New York Times* puzzle, when I sat down to construct my own puzzles, I found myself trying to worm my way out of tight spots with clues like "Mohammedan title" (HOGI). Today, I'd laugh if that clue were in a puzzle submitted to me at *Newsday* (not least because I can't even turn up any evidence now that *hogi* actually *is* a Mohammedan title). But I was keen to become a constructor, and I intended to blunder my way to success. After coming up with a few puzzles that seemed at least adequate, I had the temerity to try to sell them—or at least to send them to editors who already knew me and who might offer some advice on how I might improve, or counsel me not to quit my day job.

I made my first sale, of the fourth puzzle I'd drawn up, to of all people Mimi Raphael—who had parlayed her own crossword tournament success into a contract to edit a series of puzzle books for a major publisher. The theme of my puzzle—I know this because I am an incorrigible pack rat and still have a copy—was famous people's middle names: "Bach" (SEBASTIAN), "Lindbergh" (AUGUSTUS), etc. It wasn't a great puzzle, but Mimi was nice enough, or charitable enough, to publish it. Selling a puzzle was, in its own way, almost as exciting as winning a crossword tournament. If puzzle constructing was the real heart of crosswording, then with this first sale I had at least gained a toehold in that world. I still have a letter (Oct. 22, 1982) from Will Shortz, who was editing the puzzles at *Games* magazine, asking for a few changes but also accepting my submission—the first puzzle I sold to the magazine. Apparently I sent some of my early, terrible puzzles to the venerable Will Weng,

because he sent me a note saying, "You're showing real improvement. . . . You better watch it, or soon you'll be a professional."

With editors in those days paying $50 or so per puzzle, turning into a full-time puzzle-constructing pro would have been a financial disaster, but I was trying to figure out how I could leverage my interest in crosswords at least into some sort of side business. I started the *Crossworder's Own Newsletter* in 1983, as a clearinghouse of information and opinions, and as a platform for my own wobbly constructing efforts. It also gave me something to do on the Long Island Railroad every day as I commuted to work. I also wanted to become a crossword editor, and since I was unwilling to wait for someone to die so I might land my own regular grid (that's generally the only source of job turnover in the business), I decided that the only way I could become skilled enough as an editor—and perhaps qualify for a job someday—would be to start my own publication. I'm certain that I was able to find a solution to this career puzzle by the lateral thinking abilities I was developing in the crossword arena.

With ads in *Games* magazine and a bit of buttonholing at crossword tournaments, I managed to sign up a few dozen and then a few hundred subscribers for the *Newsletter* ($20 a year). Most readers heartily supported the darts I regularly tossed at Maleska's *Times* puzzles, but a few old-timers objected. The clash between new-wave crosswords and the Gray Lady's gray way of doing things began to crop up in articles in other publications, and I found myself being depicted (accurately) as one of the most enthusiastic of the new-wave bomb-throwers. But the most important article, for me personally, was one that ran in *Manhattan, inc.* magazine in December 1985. Writer James Kaplan (who's now at the *New Yorker* and a bestselling author) gave a vivid account of his quest to challenge me in the grid, and in the process must have made me sound like a reasonably interesting character, because after the story came out I got a call from a literary agent asking if I was interested in doing crossword books. I was *very* interested. At that point, I was the manager of the pricing and production department in the Debt Strategy Group for Merrill Lynch Capital Markets. A nice enough job, but one that lacked a certain excitement. Becoming an author of books on a subject that I was passionately interested in would be *thrilling*.

In short order, I was producing crossword collections for a top-shelf publisher, Macmillan. I also started sending my puzzles out to newspapers and magazines, with a few successes here and there, but hardly enough to make me think about quitting my day job. Then, in 1987, I suddenly didn't *have* a day job: I was among the thousands of Wall Streeters laid off in the aftermath of the stock market crash. I was unable, despite diligent efforts, to find a comparable job in finance during those grim days. At that point, what I had to do became obvious: My crossword sideline had to become

my main source of income. In my analysis, I felt my first step needed to be to become a puzzle editor for a major newspaper, so I directed my energy into trying to land the Sunday crossword slot at my local daily, *Newsday*. Thanks to a contact, reporter A. J. Carter, who had written about me in the paper, I managed to get my foot in the door with a proposal, and within a few weeks of losing my Wall Street job, I was offered the editorship of the *Newsday* Sunday puzzle. In retrospect, I realize this was a remarkable stroke of luck, given how seldom newspapers change puzzle editors. With the *Newsday* job in place, syndication seemed like a potentially lucrative way of getting more financial bang per puzzle, but my agent had no experience or interest in the syndication world. So I started shopping, in my analytical way, for someone new: I got a directory of literary agents and started writing to them. As it happened, one person I contacted was Joseph Vallely, a former book salesman who was just getting started in the agenting game. Joe shared my eagerness to see if we could shake some more money out of grid work, plus he had experience in syndication, so we began working together.

In my desperation to stay afloat after losing my job, I took out ads in *Adweek* magazine offering my services designing custom puzzles. I had heard from other constructors how lucrative it could be to design custom puzzles for corporate clients, but I wasn't getting those calls—so I decided to drum up some business for myself. And the ads worked: I did puzzles for Citibank, Johnson & Johnson,

7 UP and other companies. But it didn't take long for me to lose my taste for working with corporate clients. The problem: I had to keep explaining why the company involved couldn't be the subject of *every answer* in the puzzle. Sometimes you've gotta use pedestrian words as links, regardless of whether they have anything to do with "brand enhancement."

One day my *Adweek* notice prompted a cryptic call from someone asking if I would be interested in designing a custom puzzle for "an executive at the Seagram Company." I asked if this executive was possibly somebody named Bronfman. The Bronfman family still owned the company at that point, and I wanted to let her know that I knew. "We can't say." Then she asked me to come into their office to discuss the project. Ugh. Doing custom puzzles—or, rather, dealing with layers and layers of obsessively controlling marketing experts—was already turning out to seem like more trouble than it was worth, even when most of the business was conducted over the phone. I wasn't about to take the train into Manhattan just to discuss the possibility of doing a puzzle. But then she offered to pay me for my time.

It turned out that Charles Bronfman and his late wife, Andrea, were cooking up a birthday present for his brother (and Seagram chairman) Edgar. It sounded pretty impressive: They were having a special edition of the *New York Times* Sunday magazine printed up with Edgar on the cover and an ad for Chivas Regal whiskey

(a fine product from the Seagram distillers) on the back cover. The rich are indeed different from you and me; they can afford to get the *New York Times* to print personalized magazines for them. My job was to produce a facsimile of the *Times* Sunday puzzle that was all about Edgar Bronfman, who was an avid puzzler. I spent a couple of hours at the advertising agency that was wrangling the project, talking to the president of the agency and Mr. and Mrs. Bronfman about topics that might be good fodder for the Edgar puzzle: from current references like something about his helicopter to allusions to his childhood (one clue and answer involved a line often uttered by a rather strict teacher at the young Mr. Bronfman's private school: "Sit while it's comfortable to sit").

I was so taken with the challenge—and so pleased to know that someone of Edgar Bronfman's station in the world still appreciated the ineffable pleasures of crossword solving—that I forgot to ask how much the job would pay. I worked for a few weeks and came up with a puzzle I thought was pretty good, turned it in, and then raised the subject of my compensation. This was a terrible way of doing business, but happily the agency didn't exploit its advantage. They asked how much I'd charge. I had no idea what was appropriate. I figured that I shouldn't be bashful about valuing my work, and that I ought to think of a well-built, personalized puzzle as if it were a custom-made work of art or furniture. It had taken three weeks to construct—easily the most time I'd ever devoted to a single puzzle. I asked for $7,500 and they instantly agreed. I just as instantly wondered if I should have asked for $10,000.

It was my best deal ever for a puzzle, and I was delighted. But by then, in the late 1980s, I was actually doing quite nicely with my crossword enterprise. The *Newsletter* had about 5,000 subscribers, and I had found a lucrative sideline selling crossword books through it. But the Bronfman fee was a handsome lump sum, and I decided that this was my opportunity to address what had become an annoying aspect of being a self-employed crossword puzzle entrepreneur: friends and acquaintances and strangers who all asked the same question when they heard what I did: "Can you make a living from crossword puzzles?" I used the bulk of the Bronfman money to put a down payment on a Lincoln Town Car. It was a rolling answer, with good suspension and power steering, to the inescapable question. Yes, I could make a living from crossword puzzles. I used to call the car the Bronfmanmobile, and I drove it for 15 years.

I received a nice letter from Edgar Bronfman after his birthday—apparently, the puzzle had gone over big—and I took the opportunity to begin sending him the *Newsletter.* To my surprise, I soon started receiving orders from Mr. Bronfman, lots of them, for the crossword books listed in the *Newsletter.* Clearly, he wasn't just an occasional solver; he was ordering them by the dozen. These contributions to my book-selling business were a pleasant by-product of the birthday-puzzle project. But not quite as pleasant as the case of French wine that was delivered to our door in Massapequa Park every holiday season for years afterward, until the Bronfmans sold Seagram to Vivendi Universal in 2000. The year before that sale, I had finally met Edgar—I'd sent a note to him, on the tenth anniversary of the birthday puzzle, thanking him for his subsequent kindnesses. Soon after I sent the note, I got a call from his assistant, who said Mr. Bronfman wanted to have lunch with me.

I put on a suit and tie—even a Brooklyn guy figures that out—and went to his office in the Seagram Building. "I'm sorry," Mr. Bronfman said as we shook hands, "but my chef isn't here today, so we're going to have to eat in the cafeteria." That was a little deflating, until we went downstairs and I discovered that Edgar Bronfman's "cafeteria" was the ultra-tony Four Seasons restaurant. Over lunch, we talked about puzzles and his voracious consumption of them. Mr. Bronfman graciously introduced me to the stream of people who stopped by the table (it was easy to make small talk with architect Philip Johnson in the Seagram Building: "So, you did a nice job on this place..."). But the best touch came when we went back up to Mr. Bronfman's office and, at my request, he wrote a sweet note to my mother, who was a great admirer of his work with the World Jewish Congress.

By then I was an old hand at chatting with the rich and famous about their crossword habits. I had been hired in 1993 by Random House to run its crossword division, and I was unabashed about cornering the celebrities who trooped through the offices and quizzing them about their puzzle interests. My interest puzzled the ones who didn't do crosswords (Clint Eastwood, Jimmy Carter, Norman Mailer), but those who liked solving them always seemed eager to discuss the subject. My favorite encounter was with General Colin Powell when he was visiting his editor, Random House president Harold Evans, to talk about the project that would become his 1995 memoir, *My American Journey.* I saw General Powell coming out of Mr. Evans' office, scooted over to introduce myself, and asked if he did puzzles. "No, but my wife does."

Ah, Alma Powell. I've had her first name in the back of my mind for a long time, wishing she were more famous because her vowel-consonant-consonant-vowel formation would be extremely useful to crossword constructors. For one thing, it would enable us to come up with a new clue to replace "____ mater."

I asked General Powell if he would like to have some of Random House's crossword collections. Before he could reply, Mr. Evans—who was, in addition to running Random House, the former editor of the London *Times* and the husband of Tina Brown, then famously editing *The New Yorker*—stepped in. "We'll send them to you," he said. Obviously my time was up; he and his writer would continue their stroll and I would scurry back to my office. But apparently it's not a good idea to get between the former Chairman of the Joint Chiefs of Staff and a gift for his beloved wife. General Powell snapped: "I want to take them with me." I did indeed scurry off to my office—and then returned, under Mr. Evans' baleful glare, with an armload of crossword books. The general put them into a bag he was carrying and marched to the elevator.

One of the ironies of my working as Random House's crossword editor-in-chief and publisher: I was now in charge of *New York Times* crossword collections edited by one Eugene T. Maleska. He had passed away the same year that I started at the company, so Maleska didn't have to endure the indignity of taking calls from the pipsqueak. But his *Times* puzzle books were still in print, and when new editions came out, I was in effect editing Maleska's work in the form in which they would be seen for years to come. The phrase "spinning in his grave" was invented for situations like that.

By then, in the mid-1990s, my scheme to syndicate crosswords was rolling along rather smoothly—unlike the way it worked initially. *Newsday* had hired me as the editor of its Sunday puzzle in 1988, which was a remarkable development, given that a few years before, my bowling league cohorts considered my puzzle-construction technique something of a gutter ball. But I had learned quickly, and the fact I lived on Long Island didn't hurt with *Newsday*. Joe, my new agent, and I decided to try to sell the syndication rights to the *Newsday* puzzles. Everyone said no, except for Creators Syndicate, which said no, *but.* The president, Rick Newcombe, said that they liked my puzzles and would be interested in carrying them if I could sign up 50 papers nationwide on my own. I accepted the challenge. Using a tip I picked up from a self-help marketing book, I called just about every newspaper publisher in the country that printed a Sunday edition, told them I was a prospective advertiser, and asked if they would send me a copy of their Sunday paper. (Hey, it wasn't exactly misleading—I had a newsletter and a business reselling crossword books, and I could conceivably have decided to advertise them.) The papers gladly sent copies to me. I immediately tossed out any that were running the *New York Times* Sunday puzzle, figuring it was unlikely they'd trade in that famous brand for an upstart crossword, but there were plenty of other papers that ran puzzles of no particular distinction. Maybe the least distinguished Sunday puzzle of all was being disseminated by the folks at the Los Angeles Times Syndicate. Having been rejected by this company, I was delighted to be able to write to papers that carried their puzzles and point out the howlers regularly appearing in them. Factual mistakes, grammatical mistakes—the Los Angeles Times Syndicate's crosswords had 'em all. I still remember some of the gaffes: stop signs that were hexagons instead of octagons, Mount Rushmore featuring five faces instead of four. I promised that if the papers started using my puzzles, I'd adhere to a rather higher construction standard. I sent personalized letters to every feature editor of every paper in the country that published a non–*New York Times* Sunday crossword. I slowly started building a roster of papers that agreed to pick up my *Newsday* puzzles. My campaign involved hundreds of follow-up phone calls and a certain fanatical doggedness, but as I was an out-of-work Wall Street bond analyst, fanatical doggedness in trying to build a crossword career seemed appropriate. It took many months of cajoling and bargaining, but I gradually recruited 50 newspapers to carry the puzzle. I went back to Creators Syndicate, and Mr. Newcombe was as good as his word: They took on the *Newsday* Sunday crossword and started vending it to scores of other papers. But Creators made a request: They wanted me to produce a daily puzzle, so that the franchise would be taken more seriously.

My first customer for the daily puzzle: *Newsday*—which then, heh-heh, dropped its daily Los Angeles Times Syndicate puzzle. Going into daily crossword production was a challenge. I'd recruit a slew of puzzle constructors, paying them myself and footing the bill for the typesetting. Like everyone else, *Newsday* was just paying the meager double-digit syndicated rate for the puzzles themselves. But I was elated: It was the major victory in the battle of new-wave constructors for national respectability—*Newsday* would become the first newspaper in the country with a contemporary crossword seven days a week. I might have been a bit too starry-eyed when I agreed to the deal, because it slowly dawned on me, once the daily puzzle was up and running, that it was not exactly going to mean a financial windfall. More like a financial sinkhole. After five years, I was still losing money. It was nice to have my hand in the game as a daily crossword editor, but I was actually making a living from my work at Random House.

In late 1996, I told *Newsday* that I'd like to give up the daily routine and go back to just editing the Sunday puzzle. They asked me to recommend a replacement, and you can be sure that I didn't mention that bastion of accuracy from L.A.

A few weeks after my daily puzzle stopped running, the phone rang. It was *Newsday*'s Bob Keane—a big cheese at the paper. His first words: "Stan, the wallpaper is peeling." Huh? The paper, he said, had received more than 1,000 calls, e-mails, and letters demanding that *Newsday* reinstate my puzzle. This was heady stuff, but what really delighted me was hearing the phrase that Mr. Keane uttered next, one that people just don't get to hear often enough in life: "What will it take for you to come back?"

We negotiated a deal that, let's just say, made it easier for me to leave Random House a few years later after the management and I started to have "creative ____________."

And so now most of my time is devoted to the *Newsday* puzzle. As a sideline, I organize annual "crossword cruises" through Holland America Line. They're a fun way to hang out with fellow

crossword enthusiasts, giving them individual attention to improve their skills, showing them how to construct puzzles, and challenging them with puzzles tied to the ship itself (which I visit before we sail so I can devise a sort of scavenger hunt, sending players in search of, say, the signature on a painting in the main dining room). And the cruises are a nice way for me to take a working vacation that my wife, Marlene, can also enjoy. [For more info on my annual cruise, see the Afterword on page 141.]

I'm also still in the book business: publishing crossword collections, but also working on crossword reference books—the flagship of that effort being *The Million Word Crossword Dictionary,* which was published in 2004 and quickly became Amazon.com's best-selling hardcover crossword reference work. As the title suggests, compiling a book of this scope was a massive undertaking, and not one I could tackle alone. Luckily, for detail-intensive projects like that, I have a collaborator, Dan Stark. Dan is a true double threat, an experienced puzzle editor/constructor and a virtuoso at using computers to manage giant reams of information. You wouldn't suspect it from meeting him: Dan is a bear of a man and lives with his wife, Roz, in a picturesque lakeside village in central Mexico.

I met Dan thanks to Will Shortz, after asking Will several years ago to recommend puzzle constructors, feeling that my stable of contributors was getting a bit thin. Dan soon became a regular contributor, one of a small group of puzzlemakers I rely on for most of the *Newsday* crosswords. The contributors do a fixed number of puzzles per month, and they tend to specialize in either early-in-the-week easier puzzles, or the later, harder ones (more about the Monday-to-Sunday progression later). "Easy" and "hard," that is, for the solver. For constructors, making the easy puzzles is just as difficult as cluing the harder puzzles. It's a constant battle to resist the ingenious—in other words, to tamp down every instinct that makes a constructor get into the business in the first place. But the real challenge is the restriction on vocabulary, trying to choose words that you're sure everyone knows, and the need to avoid any but the most obvious factual clues. You come up with a seemingly stone-cold obvious clue, thinking that no one could be so badly educated or plain ignorant that they'd be stymied by it—and then an image floats up of the blank-faced guy across the counter at the car-rental office, or the uncomprehending woman who took your call yesterday when you ill-advisedly tried to ask a simple question about your cable TV service . . . and then you consider whether that Monday puzzle clue couldn't be made a wee bit simpler.

One of the pitfalls of working on the easier puzzles is that, because you're by definition not getting too obscure with your cluing, you often rely on facts that you think you know off the top of your head. If you need to look it up, then it must be too arcane for a Monday puzzle, right? That's almost always where factual errors creep into puzzles. Out of 30,000 clues per year in the *Newsday*

puzzles I edit, there might be three or four errors—not a bad ratio, I guess, but it's still intolerable when you're shooting for perfection. Several years ago, I referred in a puzzle to the Blue Angels as Air Force flyers; I was strafed the next day with more than 100 e-mails telling me that they're part of the Navy. I was chagrined, of course, but also impressed: These veterans are a proud bunch. And rightfully so.

Most of the notes I receive pointing out mistakes are polite. Not all of the freelance fact-checkers in the now worldwide *Newsday* crossword audience are so civilized. Thankfully, the most abusive notes almost always come from know-it-alls who invariably turn out to know less-than-all. It's a keen pleasure to reply with an extremely diplomatic correction of their boneheaded attempt at a correction.

E-mail has fostered much more interaction between puzzle editors and readers. When I started editing *Newsday*'s puzzle in the 1980s, readers who took the trouble to write a letter and send it to the paper complaining, say, that my use of "stat" for "statistic" ought to be clued as an abbreviation, were relatively rare. (*No,* because "stat" is a shortened form of the word, not an abbreviation.) Now it's the work of a moment to fire off an e-mail message to the puzzle editor, and plenty of readers do. I like the exchanges, because it's enjoyable to compare notes with fellow puzzle enthusiasts, and because any sort of feedback, even the notes from Mr.

Indignant, are evidence that people care about your work—that you're not just sending it off into the ether every day.

There is always at least a handful of e-mail from readers when I check my inbox at about six every morning. But before I sit down at the computer, first I look at *Newsday* and check the puzzle, just to make sure there hasn't been a printing error. The puzzle in that day's paper is the product of a three-month editing process. I select a month's worth of puzzles at a time, from those submitted by my regular contributors and a handful that came in over the transom, in addition to the one per week that I know I'll create myself. If February's puzzles are coming back from the typesetter for final review, March's are at the typesetter being readied for publication, and April's are being examined by my eagle-eyed assistant before I do my work and send them to the typesetter as electronic files.

When I'm looking at a puzzle for the first time to see if it's one I might use, I check the theme first to see if it's intriguing, and I keep an eye out for obscure or inappropriate words. Those might be words that could hurt someone's feelings, like "cripple," or just seem needlessly crass, like "idiot." Most constructors realize that crosswords have to display a certain amount of decorum. The use of pointlessly obscure words is more commonplace. Puzzle-making is mindbendingly difficult, and it's awfully tempting, when you're tired and frustrated, to just let your guard down and convince yourself that if you spot people a letter or two, they'll know that

QUECHUA is the language of the Incas. I might let QUECHUA through as an answer in a Saturday puzzle, but if it's in a puzzle that's otherwise pegged toward a Monday or Tuesday, then I'll tweak it so that the answer still begins with a consonant and ends with consonant-consonant-vowel-vowel, but the answer is GYM SHOE. Another example: TESS, as in "of the D'Urbervilles" would be fine for a Wednesday puzzle, but on Monday or Tuesday she becomes NESS of Loch or *Untouchables* fame. Most of the puzzles I receive are pitched toward the middle of the week, and my job is to push them up or back on the Hard/Easy meter.

Fine-tuning a crossword involves poring over the puzzle, fact-checking, and examining it for the thousands of ways it could go wrong, from simple mistakes like the verb tense of the clue not agreeing with the tense required in the answer ("Adds to" is asking for AUGMENTS), to clues lacking enough clarity for my taste. A constructor might think that "Before rate or time" is a deft way of cluing PRIME, but that formulation bugs me—are we talking about "before" as in "prior to" or "positioned in front of?" It's gratuitously confusing. The edited clue becomes "Word before rate or time."

Every editor has particular obsessions. In addition to my fanaticism about not using ridiculously obscure words, I'm a stickler about the answers for theme puzzles uniformly conforming to the theme. I know where the obsession comes from: During Maleska's day at the *Times*, it wasn't unusual to see a supposedly theme puzzle call for a grouping like this: FRENCH TOAST, BELGIAN WAFFLE, ENGLISH MUFFIN, and BOSTON BAKED BEANS. It sort of works, except the first three answers refer to countries, and the last one to a city. Moreover, the first three use the place names in adjectival form, while the last is in noun form. In order to be parallel, the fourth answer would have to be "Bostonian Baked Beans," and Boston would have to secede from the Union.

Nowadays, the *Times* puzzles under Will Shortz's direction are impeccable, so that sort of gaffe is unheard of, but mistakes I encountered back in the days when I was just a solver, not a constructor or editor, made me acutely alert when I started vetting *Newsday* puzzles.

Being a crossword puzzle editor for a major American newspaper, I found when I was hired, does not require the editor's presence at the newspaper's offices. At first, I thought that was too bad. I kind of like the idea of working away on my grids while scenes from a modern-day *Front Page* unfold around me, but I suspect that these days newspaper employees, like most office workers, operate by instant messages, phone calls, and the occasional meeting. Instead of my looking up from trying to wrestle the clues for a Friday puzzle into shape as hard-bitten editors bark at young reporters to race over to the fire on Main Street and sports writers regale each other with tales from locker room interviews, it would just be a lot of quiet tap-tap-tapping on keyboards and muffled phone conversations from the other side of the cubicle wall. So I'm content with my solitary work in the office we added to our house in Massapequa Park a few years ago, with lots of shelves for all my reference books. I don't see my puzzle collaborators very frequently—most live in other towns and communicate by e-mail, and even my assistant lives miles away and is seldom seen.

I have more frequent contact with my Tuesday-night word-game group. Soon after my *Newsday* puzzle began appearing in 1988, I got a call from someone asking, "Are you that guy who does the puzzles?" The person on the other end asked if I'd like to join a small group of folks who were getting together regularly to play word games.

I hesitantly agreed to stop by the following week. I drove to the address in nearby Wantagh, half imagining a horror-film plot featuring a newly hired puzzle editor lured to his death by solvers enraged over their favorite newspaper puzzle's being handed to an interloper. But, happily, it turned out that the couple who had invited me, George and Dorothy Bredehorn, were not going cruciverballistic, and I began a rewarding relationship with a bunch of people (usually about half a dozen) who are just as intoxicated with words and wordplay as I am. I was the first professional crossworder in the group, but I was delighted a few years ago when the person who had originally invited me to join, Fred Piscop—who had been working for a defense contractor on Long Island until he got laid off—was hired as the editor of the *Washington Post*'s Sunday puzzle.

So Fred went from making weapons to making puzzles—now that's my idea of beating swords into plowshares. Which reminds me: That Biblical phrase about swords/plowshares comes from the Book of Joel. I should keep the passage in mind the next time I'm working on a Saturday puzzle and need a clue for a certain four-letter word beginning with the letter J. If it's a Monday puzzle, of course, I'd have to go with "Singer Billy."

CHAPTER THREE

Inside the Grid: Basic Rules and 100 Essential Words

"I'm not good at crosswords." I've heard it hundreds of times, usually half a second after I've explained to strangers what I do for a living. Then I try to quiz them to find out if they actively dislike crossword puzzles, or if they just think they don't have the skill for solving them. Because there's a big difference. I'm prejudiced, but if they hate crossword puzzles, I'm tempted to say that they hate life. Or at least the life of the mind. Maybe they're adrenaline junkies who can't tolerate a pursuit that doesn't require you to get off the couch to do the pursuing. That's fine—with such folks, I happily leave them to their naked hang-gliding or Ironman Triathlons, and I return to a pastime that requires plenty of nimbleness but rarely causes bruising.

But if the I'm-not-good-at-crosswords strangers avoid puzzling because they think they simply lack the knack, I say: Don't despair.

It reminds me of people who say they can't ice skate because they have "weak ankles." Almost invariably, the truth is that they have weak skates. Most puzzlephobes are not "bad" at crossword puzzles, they just don't have the tools essential for making the sort of quick progress that produces a lifelong devotion to solving. Unlike almost every other game, crossword puzzles don't come with a set of instructions. Infuriating, no? Novice solvers certainly could use a briefing on how best to tackle crosswords, but even experienced solvers might profit from hearing about basic rules and strategy—who knows, maybe you've been needlessly struggling for years over certain aspects of your game and were just unaware that a better approach existed.

As I've mentioned in passing, the *Newsday* puzzles that I edit—as with the fabled *New York Times* crossword—become progressively harder as the week unfolds. I used to assume that this arrangement was understood even by occasional solvers, but I've seen dumbfounded reactions to this news often enough that I feel constrained to make it clear. My policy is that Monday's puzzle should be solvable for a high school student—an average student, not a National Merit Scholar—and for inexperienced adult solvers. With each passing day, as the difficulty level increases (with longer words and less obvious factual references, but also with trickier clues for simpler words that could appear any day). This approach has become a tradition in many newspapers because it's the only way to insure that solvers of every ability level will face a puzzle

that's just right for them at some point during the week. Saturday's puzzle, which I call the Saturday Stumper, might not always be of championship-caliber difficulty, but it should make even a talented solver sweat a few bullets. Many people who work only on Sunday puzzles assume—because the puzzle is bigger, and because you hear so much about the *New York Times* Sunday puzzle as a sort of paragon of the puzzling art—that they're solving the hardest puzzle the paper can throw at them. They're crestfallen when I break the news that the difficulty level on Sundays is about the same as a Wednesday or Thursday puzzle. It just takes longer to solve, but that's a good thing when you're having fun.

Solving *any* puzzle will be more time-consuming than necessary if you don't pause a moment before starting and take look at its title. Unlike the titles of Hollywood movies, which often seem like the interchangeable products of focus-group sessions, puzzle titles actually tell you something about the product. They're there to give you a hint at the puzzle's theme. I said *hint*—they're not exactly gimmes. Often, they'll seem innocuous and obvious enough, only to turn out to mean something completely different from what you first assumed. Seeing the title "Let's Deal," you could very well then buckle down to solving the puzzle thinking that the theme answers (usually the longest ones in the puzzle) will have something to do with business transactions of some kind. But then, as the wording of the theme answers begins to be unveiled by the crossing words, you detect that the puzzle's actually about card games. Maybe the next day the title of the puzzle is "Go Fish," and you think: *Wait a minute, we just did card games; it must be about varieties of fish.* Ah, yes, but "fish" can be a noun or a verb, and in this case the constructor's talking about fish*ing*—and the theme answers are phrases such as BY HOOK OR BY CROOK and ROD SERLING. If you were tricked by your initial reading of the title, don't carp about it, just get back to work.

The *Times* only puts titles on its Sunday puzzles, which I think is unfortunate, because it forfeits the opportunity on other days of the week to add a fillip of wordplay to the solving and to bring a smile to solvers' faces once they've figured out the connection between the title and the theme. I put a title on every *Newsday* puzzle for those reasons, and because the title might be extremely helpful to an otherwise stymied solver; I don't ever want people to give up mid-puzzle. It happens, of course, but this knowledge pains me. Except on Saturdays. Then you're on your own. I certainly don't set out to make the Saturday Stumper impossible to solve, and in fact I think that most crossword fans would be able to complete it if they devote enough time and attention to it. But the Saturday Stumper ain't easy. Did I say that I put titles on every *Newsday* puzzle? I meant to say that I do a new one for every puzzle except the Saturday Stumper—which is always called the Saturday Stumper because, well, there's never a theme that would warrant a more informative title.

You'll find three to five theme answers in most daily puzzles, and eight to twelve of them on Sundays. For the big Sunday puzzle, I provide an additional blurb with the title to help things along. To a puzzle called "WW II," I added: "Having nothing to do with armed conflict." The theme was two-word phrases in which both words started with the letter W, as in WISHING WELL and WATER WORKS. Another Sunday puzzle bore the title "Horse Play," with the blurb "Getting off the track." I wanted to let solvers know that the theme would have something to do with equine matters, but that it would be coming at the subject from an odd angle. Hence the clue "Gourmet horse food?" would be galloping toward the answer GRAND FODDER. The presence of a question mark, by the way, signals the need for a wordplay answer.

(I know, I know, puns get a bad press in many quarters, but in the crossword world we love 'em. The more outrageous the better. Besides, are puns really so terrible as a genre of humor? They mean no harm, they're intended purely to amuse, and they reflect the pun-maker's affection for the language. I sometimes get the feeling that puns have been unfairly maligned by people *who simply don't get them,* and that this anti-pun faction has complained so publicly for so long that it has become conventional wisdom to believe that all puns are bad puns, and that all pun-makers are unfunny bores. To admit that you like puns is to risk having the world think that you, too, are an unfunny bore. I suspect that many people harbor a secret shame, feeling constrained to groan about "bad" puns when they're around others, even though, deep down, they're tickled to death. To them I say: Don't be ashamed, don't be a sheep—the crossword world will accept ewe.)

Ignoring the title of a crossword puzzle, then, is to deprive yourself of a useful tool in deciphering the puzzle's theme. Yet many people indeed skip the title and just plunge into the grid. That's Common Mistake Number One. Number Two: tackling the puzzle by starting at 1 Across, with the intention of proceeding through the clues in order. You're certainly welcome to work this way, but as the wise man said, the path to puzzle happiness is a winding one, Grasshopper. Since you're free to answer any clue anywhere in the Across and Down columns, scan them for an obvious, easy clue—one you're absolutely sure of. It could very well be 1 Across, but don't get bogged down there (and it could very well *not* be 1 Across; constructors make no special effort to make that clue easier or harder). Very often, fill-in-the-blank clues—"Gone With the ____" (WIND) or "From ___ Z" (A TO)—are ones that you can be most certain of solving correctly. At the risk of lapsing into pop-psychologyspeak (shrink rap?), I'd say that achieving an immediate success in the grid builds confidence. But there's a more concrete benefit: The first answer you jot down will be become the building block of every crossing word it touches, and since you're almost certain it's correct, the chances of a wrong answer for a crossing word are substantially reduced.

The methodical "Start at 1 Across" approach is a game of Russian roulette, unless the first clue is in fact as easy as "Game of Russian ________," because you're answering in a vacuum. Without crossing words providing a letter or two to insure your accuracy, if 1 Across is "Type of fruit," asking for a four-letter answer, you could very well enter PEAR or LIME, with no way of knowing which is correct. In that way misery lies, because if the clue for 1 Down is "Body of water," calling for another four-letter answer, the solver who put down PEAR for 1 Across would answer POOL as the body of water, while the LIME person would go with LAKE. The solver who's on the wrong track—even though the answers *seem* to be working—might not figure it out until after a 20-minute session of blundering down blind alleys.

It's tempting, if you've started out well by finding an easy answer, to begin scanning the clues for other softballs so that you can sprinkle the grid with a handful of surefire answers. I don't recommend this. Experience has taught me that solving will be faster and easier if you concentrate on one area of the puzzle at a time, building as thoroughly as possible on the first answer you entered. With luck, a chain reaction of correct answers will ensue, and your solving will unfold across the grid. But if you reach an impasse, then try to colonize a nearby section of the puzzle by finding another relatively easy clue, with the intention of linking the new area to the one you were just working in. Jumping around in the puzzle might succeed in producing a few pockets of answers, but it can be more time-consuming and frustrating to try to link up this archipelago—suddenly all the relatively easy clues are gone, and you're left with just the hard ones—than to build steadily outward from a core of answers.

Not that this approach will necessarily produce a solved puzzle. As the week progresses and the difficulty level rises, your chances of stalling short of the finish line also increase. You might have half of the puzzle still open, a third, or just one section that remains a white fortress making one last stand against your onslaughts ("Remember the _____"). Faced with what appears to be a dead end, many people find themselves reading the remaining clues over and over again, refusing to give in, ratcheting up their fury with each fruitless pass. If you find yourself in this position, I say: Stop! Put the puzzle aside for a few hours or even overnight. One of the peculiar things about crosswords, as I and plenty of other devoted solvers have found, is that a clue that seemed incomprehensible in the morning can suddenly make sense if you turn to it with a fresh eye. You might torture yourself over the seeming simplicity of the clue "Pie filling," calling for a three-letter answer (*hmm, three letters, pies, pies, pies . . . don't the English eat eel pies? Doesn't fit. Starts with an M. Magpie? That's a bird. And MAG is not a filling. Grrrhr!*), but then you put the puzzle down, go for a walk, notice some children playing outside, sitting in the dirt, as children are wont to do, and—presto!—the solution comes to you: MUD pie.

Then there are the hellish clues, the ones you know in your bones that you'll never solve, like "School where Stonewall Jackson taught." If this were for a weekday or Sunday puzzle, I'd add "abbr." to the clue, just to help out a bit, but since it's a hard one to begin with, I'd probably use it only for a Saturday Stumper, with no helper). Faced with a seemingly insoluble clue like the "Stonewall" stonewall, many people will sneak a look at a dictionary or encyclopedia or Google to grab the answer so they can get back on track, but feeling guilty for cheating once they've discovered that the answer is VMI.

I'm here to say: *Don't feel guilty.* Yes, there's a much higher level of satisfaction if you can finish a crossword without the use of performance-enhancing reference works. And purists would say that's the only honest way to do puzzles. *But the essential points of doing crosswords are to have fun and learn something.* This isn't the Virginia Military Institute, and there's no crossword honor code to violate. The chagrin you feel about having to look up an answer is punishment enough; loading guilt about "cheating" on top of it is just overkill. Better to find the correct answer and have it embedded in your brain, awaiting deployment in a future puzzle, than to abandon the puzzle, wondering if Stonewall Jackson taught at SMU.

But before you peek . . . consider the possibility that if an entire section of the puzzle is unfilled except for a word or two, those answers might be wrong and preventing you from moving ahead. Erase them and consider the clues afresh. Oh, you say you can't erase because you were working in ink? *Haven't you learned anything from all the people walking around these days with tattoos that you just know they're going to regret?* Ink is unforgiving. Trying to solve a puzzle while contending with inked-in answers that you know are incorrect is tedious work and needlessly makes the solving harder. Work with a pencil. If you have an incurable show-off gene and simply must use a pen in order to impress—oh, I dunno, maybe the other people in the dermatologist's waiting room with appointments to have their tattoos removed?—then buy an erasable pen.

In addition to condoning emergency peeking for answers, I also urge solvers to consult the dictionary whenever they encounter an unfamiliar word or unusual usage. But beyond the dictionary, I recommend looking up *any* information that's new to you, so you can learn a little more context about it than can be expressed in the few words of a puzzle clue. Doing this quickie research will improve your vocabulary, widen your knowledge base, polish your crossword-solving skills, and maybe even remove stubborn kitchen stains.

When you've completed a puzzle, take another look at the title

and see how it relates to the theme. It will familiarize you with constructors' thinking when they dream up their titles, which should make it easier for you to guess the theme of the next puzzle and thus improve your solving. In fact, check the title more than once during the course of solving the puzzle—that's what many experienced solvers do, knowing that the theme they thought they discerned upon first reading the title might turn out to be something much different, once they've used crossing words to spell out a few theme answers. Armed with these words, the solver might understand the title in a completely different way.

My themeless Saturday puzzles are another matter. But since the puzzle-making process is operating at its highest level on Saturdays, if you understand how constructors think about these puzzles, you'll have much more fun deciphering the clues. Once you're attuned to the devilish complexity of the Saturday puzzles, solving on other days of the week will become radically easier.

Despite the fact that the Saturday Stumper has no theme, uses longer words, and provides clues that are better camouflaged than on other days, it's important to remember that for Saturday puzzles, in general, constructors do not artificially increase their difficulty by employing uselessly obscure or unusual words. That's subjective, of course, since one person's obscurity is another's everyday usage. I recommend erring on the side of assuming that the answer will be a word you already know, but one that might just not come readily to mind. The reason the difficulty level increases on Saturday should lie in the cluing, not in the answers themselves.

And, oh boy, do constructors love to send solvers down blind alleys and off the ends of piers. You should have your misdirection sensors activated at all times. A clue like "Fine skipper," with "fine" seeming to suggest "good" and "skipper" bringing to mind, in all likelihood, something nautical, might make you start pondering an answer like GOOD CAPTAIN or variations (ADMIRABLE ADMIRAL?). But nothing seems to work in the eight-letter space provided in the grid, so you start to reconsider. Maybe it's "skipper" as in jumping over something. Since you've still got water on the brain from your nautical excursion, it would be easy to segue into trying the answer FLAT ROCK—hey, a flat rock is fine for skipping, and it's eight letters . . . but it doesn't work with the handful of crossing letters that you know are correct. Sigh. Okay, reset. You begin racking your brain to figure out if there's a word for a child who's especially "fine," as in talented, at "skipping," as in hopscotch. Uh, no. The problem is that you've so thoroughly bought into "fine" meaning "good" that it could be a long time—possibly until filling in all the crossing words reveals the correct answer—before you realize that in this case "fine" means monetary punishment and the eight-letter answer for a person who avoids, or skips, paying such a fine is known as a SCOFFLAW.

Some of the best misdirections are the clues that seem so plain

and simple, they couldn't possibly be hiding a constructor's black arts at work. "Government program" sounds simple enough. If it had been "Govt. program," with the abbreviation signaling that the answer will be an abbreviation as well, then it could have been that old crossword stand-by "NRA," for Roosevelt's National Recovery Administration. But this answer's not an abbreviation. WELFARE? SUBSIDY? No . . . it's an 11-letter answer. While you're riffling through your memory banks like they're the *Congressional Record*, searching for a government program that fits the bill, you're journeying so far inside the Beltway that you've left behind the possibility that "program" might not refer to *anything* governmental, and in fact could mean "program" as in "television show," like, oh, THE WEST WING.

One of my all-time favorite misdirections was the clue "They may go up in a plane." The "they" prompts you to start thinking "Who? Pilots? Passengers? Flight attendants—no, that's *way* too long! It's an eight-letter answer . . . nothing fits!" But a solver who's alert to the deviousness of constructors will constantly assess clues for alternative meanings. In this case almost every aspect of the clue is a misdirection. "They" does not necessarily refer to a group of persons. (Maybe it's the landing gear? No, we need a plural. WHEELS? That's only six letters.) "Go up" could mean something other than climbing from the runway to the sky. "In a plane" doesn't have to mean the subject of the answer will have entered the airplane for the purpose of being wedged into a thinly padded torture device for several hours. Hang on a second—let's think about those airplane seats. TRAY TABLES "go up," don't they? But that's ten letters. Sigh. What other things go up? Ahhh, yes: ARMRESTS. I'm still tickled by that one. It was a clue for a Saturday Stumper, so I couldn't go with anything obvious. Initially I thought about living room furniture, but that wasn't very promising so I let my mind wander. This blue-sky thinking, so to speak, led me to airplanes and to a clue that definitely requires solvers to use some mental elbow grease.

When performing your misdirection detection, be wary of part-of-speech ambiguity. Verbs like "put" and "set" can be either present or past tense. "Put away" could mean EAT or ATE, STOW or STOWED. "Quit" could be GIVE UP or GAVE UP. Puzzle editors live for this stuff. And our affection for wildlife, or at least their ambiguous numbering—is that one or two FISH, a singleton DEER or a herd of them?—practically qualifies us for honorary PETA memberships. The best policy is to be suspicious of every clue: Never trust your first impression. Many words and phrases have multiple meanings, and puzzle constructors, in their wickedness, love to exploit the instincts of good and trusting solvers. Words like "run" (operate or dash?), "come to" (arrival or wake up or add up to?) and "break" (noun or verb?) might seem obvious in their meanings, but they're not. Obviously. Take a clue like "You can't stand to have them." A solver's perfectly understandable first impulse might be to start thinking of all the things he or she finds irksome that one might "have"—though that verb already lends a little trickiness. "Have" as in have over your tedious in-laws for a wasted weekend afternoon? Or "have" as in have audits by the IRS? Or "have" as in have the measles? (And would measles qualify as a plural "them," or is it an illness, singular?) While you're thus engaged, you're neglecting to challenge the meaning of "stand," which in this case simply means to be no longer sitting. So the answer to this question about those which you cannot stand in order to have is actually rather simple: LAPS (let's argue some other time about whether the clue should have read "You can't stand to have it" because one does not have a series of laps so much as one lap that comes or goes. On this laps question, you could go around and around forever. Oops, there's another meaning of the word, NASCAR fans. Would have been a mental lapse not to mention it.)

As with "You can't stand . . . ," the meanings of familiar phrases of every type are twisted beyond all recognition by puzzle constructors. Solvers could be excused for reading the clue "It sticks to your ribs" and drifting into a reverie about particularly filling meals they've enjoyed. But the ribs in question are not those surrounding your internal organs, they're the ones on your plate. And BARBECUE SAUCE is what sticks to them.

Another weapon in the constructor's arsenal, of course, has nothing to do with parts of speech, ambiguous meanings, or any other gray area of language. It's just the facts. Facts that, more often than not, you're already acquainted with in some way. Sometimes the clues and answers touch on a field of knowledge that's simply not part of your experience and you have no chance of getting the answer right except by piecing it together with crossing words. In most cases, though, clues call for answers that refer to perfectly familiar words or names, but in unusual or unfamiliar contexts. "Builder of the first Madison Square Garden" might seem awfully obscure—probably some now-forgotten architect from a century ago—but then the answer emerges from the crossing letters: BARNUM. The clue "Literally, 'jumping flea'" doesn't require a knowledge of entomology in order to be answered; it's the actual meaning in Hawaiian of UKULELE. A constructor who wants to employ the answer ASTAIRE in a grid, but who would like to make the clue more difficult than, say, "*Top Hat* star" or "Rogers' partner," might opt for one that really tests the solvers' pop-culture knowledge: "*The Towering Inferno* Oscar nominee."

Beyond all the fact-based troubles that constructors throw your way, and all the fiendish wordplay and misdirection, there is another category of clues and answers that is simply a necessary evil of the business. These are the short words with the perfect arrangement of consonants and vowels that constructors rely on as the connective tissue for their puzzles. Yes, these words flirt with deplorable obscurity. Many of them even qualify as crosswordese. But have

pity for constructors: Sometimes we get desperate, especially if we've got a killingly funny clue-and-answer going Across and it's essential to have the YSER River flowing Down. In my defense, I'll point out that at *Newsday*, I've imposed a three-per-puzzle limit on their usage, which is very rarely reached. Crossword-making software now offers the constructor so many good choices for answers that even my three-per-puzzle limit now seems too generous. It's a pity that many of those people who say they're "not good at crosswords" base this perception on a long-ago unhappy experience with puzzles back when crosswordese was much more prevalent in the business. That certainly has changed. I admit, though, that these words can play a critical role in building a puzzle; being familiar with them is vital to becoming a highly skilled puzzle solver. And so, even though I have a deep-down aversion to them, here's my list of **100 Essential Words** that crossworders need to know, with two common clues for each.

ADA—Oklahoma city; Toothpaste-approving org.

ADEN—Mideast gulf; City of Yemen

ADIT— Mine entrance; Horizontal passage

ADO—Fuss; Ruckus

AGA—Turkish title; __ Khan

AGAR—Ice cream ingredient; Culture medium

AGEE—*The African Queen* screenwriter; 1969 Mets hero

ALAI—Jai __; Eurasian mountain range

ALAR—Winglike; Banned apple spray

ALEE—Away from the wind; Nautical adverb

ALI—Three-time heavyweight champ; Actress MacGraw

ALIT—Landed; Touched down

ALOE—Spiny houseplant; Lotion ingredient

AMO— I love: Lat.; Start of a Latin trio

ANA— Literary miscellany; Santa __, California

ANON—Of unknown authorship: Abbr.; Poetic adverb

A-ONE—First-rate; Top-notch

APSE—Church feature; Altar neighbor

ARA—Altar constellation; Football coach Parseghian

ARAL—Caspian Sea neighbor; Asian sea

ARES—Greek war god; Son of Zeus

ARI—Nickname of Onassis; *Exodus* character

ARLO—Singer Guthrie; Woody's son

ARNE—"Rule, Britannia" composer; "Judith" composer

ARNO—River of Florence; *The New Yorker* cartoonist

ARTE—Commedia dell'__; Comedian Johnson

ASEA—Between ports; On a cruise

ASHE—Arthur of tennis; 1975 Wimbledon winner

ASTA—*The Thin Man* dog; Nick and Nora's pet

AVER—State with certainty; Attest

CREE—Canadian Indian; Manitoba native

EAVE—Roof overhang; Icicle site

ECRU—Brown color; Hosiery shade

EDIE—Singer Adams; Singer Brickell

EDO—Tokyo's former name; Nigerian people

EEE—Wide shoe; Shoebox letters

EER—Auction suffix; Poetic adverb

EGAD—Old-time exclamation; "Zounds!"

EIRE—England neighbor; Word on Irish coins

EKE—__ out a living; Supplement, with "out"

ELAN—Gusto; Enthusiasm

ELIA—Director Kazan; Lamb's pen name

ELIE—Author Wiesel; Composer Siegmeister

ELLE—Fashion magazine; French pronoun

ELSA—*Born Free* lioness; Actress Lanchester

EMIR—Ruler of Kuwait; Moslem leader

ENE—Compass pt.; Chemical suffix

ENID—City in Oklahoma; Author Bagnold

ENOS—Son of Seth; Hazzard County deputy

EON—Geological period; Very long time

EOS—Dawn goddess; Aurora alias

EPEE—Fencing sword; Olympics weapon

ETE—French summer; When Paris sizzles

ERE—Before, in poems; Palindromic preposition

ERG—Unit of work; Joule fraction

ERLE—__ Stanley Gardner; Perry's creator

ERNE—Sea eagle; Fish-eating flier

EROS—Greek love god; Cupid alias

ERSE—Gaelic; Celtic language

ESAU—Jacob's twin; Birthright seller

ESSE—To be: Lat.; Latin existence

ESTE—Villa d'__; Italian princely surname

ETAL—Footnote abbr.; And others, for short

ETNA—Sicilian volcano; Lab heater

ETON—British prep school; School founded by Henry VI

ETRE—Raison d'__; To be: Fr.

ETTA—Kett of comics; Sundance Kid's girlfriend

ETUI—Needle case; Sewing kit

EWER—Water pitcher; Carafe kin

IAGO—Shakespearean villain; Othello foe

ILE— __ de France; Suffix for percent

INRE—Concerning; About

IOTA—Greek vowel; Tiny amount

NEA—Teachers' org.; PBS benefactor

NEE—Society page word; Born: Fr.

NENE—Hawaii state bird; Oahu goose

OBI—Japanese sash; __-Wan Kenobi

ODIN—Norse god; Father of Thor

OLE—Bullfight cheer; Grand __ Opry

OLEO—Butter alternative; Margarine

OLIO—Miscellany; Hodgepodge

OLLA—__ podrida; Spanish stewpot

ORE—Mine find; Metallic rock

OREL—Pitcher Hershiser; City on the Oka

ORO—Gold: Sp.; Conquistador's quest

ORR—Bobby of hockey; Bruins great

OTT—Mel of baseball; Giant Hall-of-Famer

RANI—Princess of India; Rajah's wife

REO—Classic car; __ Speedwagon

SERE—Dried up; Parched

SLOE—Plumlike fruit; __ gin fizz

SRO—Broadway sign; Box office letters

STE—Fr. holy woman; Sault __ Marie

STET—Proofreader's mark; Don't dele

TESS—Thomas Hardy girl; Mrs. Dick Tracy

TSAR—Former Russian ruler; Absolute monarch

ULNA—Arm bone; Radius neighbor

URAL—Caspian Sea feeder, Russian mountain range

UTE—Western Indian; Salt Lake City collegian

YSER—Belgian river; North Sea feeder

Yes, I know: It's a long list of words you just don't find yourself using much on a day-to-day basis. Here's a mnemonic that probably won't be any help at all . . .

There once was a young man from Ada who went to Aden exploring for gold, but then at the adit an ado erupted when the Aga Khan intervened, saying, "It's not gold in there, it's agar." The young man thought, "What would Tommie Agee do?" He decided to repair to the Alai, flying on an alar device of his own making, which required steering alee if he wanted to float like the butterfly of Ali fame. Then he alit, landing on an aloe plant, and said, "Ouch! Amo that? I think not."

. . . On second thought, feel free to complete this story yourself. I just wanted to get it started, so you wouldn't be stuck up the Yser without an Orr.

CHAPTER FOUR

Crossword History: From the World*'s First to Java 1.4.2*

Liverpool's two greatest gifts to the world of popular culture are the Beatles and Arthur Wynne. No doubt you're familiar with the former; the latter is the giant among men who gave us the crossword puzzle. Born in 1862, Wynne immigrated to the United States as a young man and—in another bit of trendsetting that continues to this day—established himself as a British editor working in New York, though, alas, without a Condé Nast expense account.

In 1913, when Wynne was in charge of the *New York World*'s "Fun" section, he decided to add a new element to the riddles, anagrams, and other challenges in the December 21 edition of the Sunday paper. Wynne drew up a variation on the word-square puzzles that have been found in writing cultures going back to first-century Pompeii. In Victorian England, word squares were used to challenge kids (and adults, with the more complex puzzles) to fill in blanks with words that read the same horizontally and vertically—imagine OFF, FOE and FED boxed together. Wynne's puzzle was a peculiar, diamond-shaped grid, with no black squares, but modern crossword puzzlers would nonetheless instantly recognize the numbered boxes and clues. Rather than being divided into the Across and Down clue columns that we know today, the clues were designated by the first numbered square in the answer and the last ("2-3 What bargain hunters enjoy." SALES), but the basic DNA of the modern crossword was in place with that first puzzle—even if Wynne wasn't calling it a crossword quite yet.

I wonder if crossword puzzles would have become as massively popular as they are today—the number of crossword fans is generally estimated at about 50 million—had the puzzles continued to go by the name Wynne used for his first effort: "word cross." Within a matter of weeks, the *World*'s puzzle was renamed the "cross word," either as a result of a typesetter's error, or just editorial second thoughts. In January 1914, the *World* published a puzzle with the headline "Find the Missing Cross Words." I know this, because I happen to be the proud owner of an original of the puzzle, a gift from Will Shortz (Will, who has a staggering collection of puzzle books and artifacts, is the only person I know of who has an original of the December 21 puzzle that started our glorious business). The early history of the crossword puzzle is endlessly retold in books

and articles, but one good account can be found in Coral Amende's 2001 book, *The Crossword Obsession.*

Even though newspaper executives back in Arthur Wynne's day had to function without the benefit of consultants, marketing surveys, and readership studies—*how did these people survive?*—the *World* decided to make Wynne's puzzle a regular feature. Their decision was guided by another important development in crossword history: The irate letter to the editor when the puzzle didn't appear in the paper. After the debut of the "word cross," readers immediately began sending in their own attempts at puzzle-making. In February 1914 the paper not only published its first puzzle from an outside contributor, but also ran a puzzle with the first byline for a constructor—one Mrs. M. B. Wood.

Mrs. Wood might have been surprised to learn that, decades later, bylines for crossword constructors would hardly be a sure thing in newspapers. Most papers are conscientious about attaching the editor's name, the constructor's name, and even an e-mail address where the editor can be reached, but some publications remain strangely resistant to crediting the people who make their puzzles. As someone who syndicates to more than 100 newspapers worldwide, I'm intimately familiar with the policies and attitudes of many editors toward crossword puzzles. I regret to report that the newspaper with the most hostile attitude I've encountered is north of the border, the *Toronto Star.* Canadians pride themselves on their inclusiveness and tolerance and lots of other buzzwordy synonyms for niceness, but the folks at their largest national daily are decidedly intolerant of the idea that each crossword puzzle is a distinct accomplishment, and that the persons who created it and edited it merit at least some small public credit (how long would the paper keep its reporters if they didn't get a byline?). Take a look at your local paper—does it give bylines to every column, feature, and comic strip but not to the crossword puzzle? You'd be doing crossword professionals everywhere a big favor if you called up the paper or shot them an e-mail and offered a not-too-subtle hint that the puzzle-maker and editor might deserve the same sort of recognition.

Okay, now I've got that off my chest. It's not as if, back in the early days, despite giving Mrs. M. B. Wood a byline, the *New York World* exactly put crosswords on a pedestal. When *World* editor John O'Hara Cosgrove decided that Wynne needed some help handling the paper's puzzle—Wynne was trying to construct puzzles, edit them, and cope with a growing deluge of outside submissions—Cosgrove assigned his secretary to the task. Margaret Petherbridge, a 1919 graduate of Smith College, initially was responsible for just making sure the crosswords were published free of mistakes, a chore she approached indifferently because she didn't happen to be too interested in crosswords. But then, once Petherbridge started solving the puzzles, she became enamored of them (love at first

cite?) and began pondering ways to make crosswords more fun and challenging.

It was a watershed moment in puzzle history, because Margaret Petherbridge was a crossword genius. Anyone seriously interested in the crossword business regards her with a certain awe, not least because many folks making puzzles today had the pleasure of knowing her: Margaret Farrar (in 1926 she married John Farrar, founding member of the Farrar, Straus and Giroux publishing house) died in 1984 at age 87, and was working on the 134th volume in the original crossword series that she started in 1924. By the time she passed away, Margaret had established many, if not most, of the rules that govern crosswords. She threw out Wynne's double-numbering of clues, decreed that the puzzles would be a symmetrical grid with no lonely patches of isolated answer squares, and laid down plenty of other rules. But her biggest contribution might have been the fact that she made ingenuity a hallmark of the crossword puzzle. She jettisoned obvious cluing, introduced the idea of theme puzzles, and generally created an atmosphere that sent a message: Crosswords were smart entertainment.

The "word cross" might have been an instant hit after its 1913 debut, but that popularity was nothing compared with the mania that set in during the 1920s, after the crossword puzzle had been Petherbridgified. In 1924, two young men just starting out in the publishing business decided to see if they could capitalize on the public fascination with newspaper crosswords. Richard Simon and Max Schuster recruited Margaret Petherbridge and two associates from the *World* as editors and brought out *The Cross Word Puzzle Book* in April—under the name Plaza Publishing, because the two partners feared the book might be greeted with such derision that it would taint their fledgling Simon & Schuster enterprise. The initial printing of 3,600 copies included an inspired sales gimmick: Each book came with its own pencil. In three months' time, the book sold 40,000 copies at $1.35 apiece. Simon & Schuster had its first big success. The company rushed two more crossword books into print; by year's end, their combined sales topped 400,000.

A Flapper-era crossword-puzzle craze was now in full bloom. Clothing designers were using the crossword's black-and-white checks and a railway company furnished its cars with crossword dictionaries for puzzle-crazed passengers. The New York Public Library instituted a rule limiting patrons' dictionary use to five minutes, because crossword fans were hogging the books in search of puzzle answers. A show called *Puzzles of 1925* hit Broadway, and a popular song of the day was called "Cross Word Mama, You Puzzle Me (But Papa's Gonna Figure You Out)."

In Pittsburgh, a crossword clue calling for "a bird of the suborder of *eleutherodactyli oscines*" (Whoa! Shades of Eugene Maleska!) brought solvers flocking to the Carnegie Library in search of the answer: SPARROW. Or at least that anecdote was reported in the

New York Times—which might have covered the crossword fad but didn't happen to publish the puzzles itself. The popularity of crosswords vaulted the Atlantic in the 1920s and become a hit in Great Britain, where the puzzles morphed into the "cryptic" format, which requires a particularly acute sense of wordplay—or, more accurately, Sherlock Holmes–level word-detective work—that can leave many American solvers mystified. But even if crosswords flourished overseas before World War II, they didn't find a home at the newspaper that would become the world's best-known puzzle venue until 1942. *New York Times* publisher Arthur Hays Sulzberger reputedly had become so infatuated with the *Herald Tribune*'s puzzle that he decided his own paper should run one as well. But it was an only-on-Sunday affair for eight years, until the daily *Times* puzzle started in 1950.

A wise man, Mr. Sulzberger inaugurated the *Times* Sunday puzzle by hiring Margaret Farrar, née Petherbridge. I know you already knew she was a Petherbridge at birth; I just like to write "née," that wonderfully useful consonant/double-vowel. No doubt Margaret employed it in more than a few puzzles that were published during her tenure at the *Times*, which lasted until her retirement in 1969. During her 27-year run at the *Times*, she established that paper as the home of what amounted to a national crossword puzzle, and she secured her status as the patron saint of puzzle constructors. (I consider myself very fortunate to have gotten into the puzzle world just in time to meet Margaret. She was handing out the prizes at the Stamford tournament and the U.S. Open in 1982, when I was delighted to receive the first-place trophies from her.)

In addition to being the great lawgiver of crosswords, Margaret also had a gift for spotting talent. She developed a stable of constructors whose only shared trait was the ability to make good puzzles: Margaret's crew included several penitentiary inmates, a violinist in the New York Philharmonic, and a sea captain. Frances Hansen contributed some of the paper's best-loved puzzles from that era. Her *Times* debut in 1964 was based on Lewis Carroll's *Through the Looking Glass and What Alice Found There* and required solvers to think and spell backwards (Clue: "A well-known part of ykcowrebbaJ." Answer: EBARGTUO SHTAR EMOM EHT DNA). The puzzle reportedly took Hansen eight months to construct.

But for all of Margaret Farrar's innovative and risk-taking approach to editing puzzles, she also had a bit of the schoolmarm about her. The use of brand names in puzzles, for instance, was strictly taboo. Her successor in the late 1960s, Will Weng, appropriately for the times, if not the *Times*, loosened the rules—with spectacular results. Puzzles published in the 1970s with Weng's imprimatur still prompt new-wave constructors to marvel at their inspired sense of humor and eagerness to test established rules. Merl Reagle credits a *Times* puzzle during the Weng era, when Merl was in his 20s, as one of his biggest influences. The puzzle was called "Thanksgiving

Fare," which sounded rather pedestrian—until the solving began, and it became evident that the answers were for food that would constitute only a fair Thanksgiving: INSTANT POTATOES, FREEZE-DRIED COFFEE, CANNED PEAS, etc.

Though some crossword fans griped that Weng prized puzzle themes so highly that he allowed too much crosswordese if it was in the service of a really inspired theme answer, you never heard a cross word about the man himself. I came on the scene a few years after Weng's tenure ended in 1977, but he was still a much-beloved presence in the puzzle world—if anything, people grew even fonder of Weng and his love for fun and wordplay after his retirement, because then the black cloud of Eugene Maleska descended on the *Times* puzzle. With Maleska in charge, the puzzle was plunged into the grim era I described in Chapter One. Maleska was the sort of editor who would have looked at the first crossword ever published, the groundbreaking puzzle from the *World* in 1913, and thought the best part of that otherwise easy puzzle was the clue "Fibre of the gomuti palm." Clearly Arthur Wynne resorted to this useless obscurity because he was desperate for a certain crossing answer. Not that the very same answer to that clue couldn't also appear in a puzzle today. But in the post-Maleska era, when the sense of fun and ingenuity from the Farrar-Weng regimes was restored and new wave constructors took puzzles to a fresh level of relevance and inspired entertainment, the gomuti-palm-fibre clue would have been thrown out and a new clue installed: "Homer Simpson exclamation": DOH.

The modern era of crosswords has a few other hallmarks as well. One is crosswords' migration into the technological age. Until recently, the way people got their puzzles and solved them had remained unchanged since the time when Richard Simon and Max Schuster provided a pencil with their first crossword book. For decades, solvers found a puzzle in the newspaper or in a book, picked up a pencil, and got down to work. That remained pretty much the case even as the computer age saw the advent of crossword-making software in the 1980s: Puzzles might have been drawn up on a computer, but they were still solved the old-fashioned way. The advent of the Internet, of course, meant that you could begin solving online—and many people do. The Web site bestcrosswords.com had 130,372 registered users the last time I checked. (Old crossword-solving paradigm: a Sunday morning spent with a puzzle and a cup of java. New crossword paradigm: a puzzle and Java 1.4.2.) A problem with Internet solving is the lack of portability. One of the attractions of crossword puzzles is that they are so loyal and companionable. You can take a folded-up piece of newsprint with you anywhere, from the sofa to the bathroom to the front porch, to the doctor's office, on the bus or an airplane, and there's your old crossword friend, still teasing you with a bit of wordplay that you haven't quite deciphered, flattering you with a few clues

that look difficult but aren't, tormenting you with ones that may not ever give up their secrets. You can put it away, take it up again, stow it away, and yet the puzzle's always there, patiently awaiting your concentrated attentions.

The lack of portability with techno-crosswords has been addressed—to a degree—by handheld devices like the New York Times Company's touch-screen crossword-puzzle device, made by Excalibur Electronics. It works with a stylus, stores a thousand puzzles, and costs about 50 bucks. Crosswords are also being delivered to cell phones and PDAs. But these electronic crossword platforms have not solved a problem much bigger than the portability question, and that's the need to reimagine crossword puzzles for the digital age. Here you have fantastic potential for bringing crosswords into the 21st century, and yet the evidence indicates that the old-fashioned approach to puzzles has just been gussied up with a few electronic bells and whistles; old-style puzzles are being shoehorned into new technologies. And, truth be told, the screens of cell phones and PDAs are pathetic venues for crossword puzzles—they're too small, and the image resolution is atrocious.

We're nowhere near exploiting the advantages offered by the microchip over newsprint. If I could have just one more new career in puzzledom, I would love it to be as the person who truly reinvented crosswords for the digital age. A sort of Arthur Wynne 2.0. I'm reluctant to discuss my ideas in much detail, because I know that others in the puzzle world are thinking along the same lines, and someday someone's going to find a financial backer to try to make it happen. I'd like to think that I might get the chance, so there's no advantage to handing free tips to the competition. But here's an idea I'll throw out. No effort has been made to exploit the most basic characteristic of the Internet: its connectivity. Why not recruit corporate sponsors and inaugurate the Super Bowl of all crossword competitions with a simultaneous crossword-solving competition open to the entire world? It's logistically possible, it might generate a tremendous amount of interest, and it could be a heck of a lot of fun.

But the most important aspect of such a major online event—and of other innovations that place crosswords firmly in the digital present—is that it might help stir interest in crosswords in a new generation of solvers. And let's tell the truth: The crossword business needs to do anything it can to recruit younger solvers, and to keep its hold on the interest of established fans. Crossword puzzles are primarily a newspaper-based pastime, and I'm not exactly making a stop-the-presses announcement by saying that newspapers are facing a dodgy future. I'm sure they'll exist, in one form or another, for decades to come, but there's no denying that newspapers are more than ever a medium with an aging fan base. Twentysomethings and even thirtysomethings just don't turn to newspapers for information as they have in the past, and that means these folks

also aren't stumbling onto the crossword and experiencing that serendipitous moment where they start solving a puzzle, the inevitable delight sets in, and they wonder where the crossword's been all their lives.

I have no doubt that crossword puzzles will still have tens of millions of fans on the centennial of their invention in 2013, but I'm not so sure about their bicentennial. Dramatic efforts, and lots of imagination, have to be devoted to relaunching the crossword puzzle for the modern age. If that happens, I suspect that the 2020s could see a revival of excitement about crosswords that recalls the puzzlemania of the 1920s.

Obviously, I want puzzle devotees to remain devoted, and the uninitiated to become initiated to the pleasures of the grid. That was my attitude when I first caught the crossword fever more than 20 years ago, but since then I have become, if anything, an even more avid crossword proponent. Here's why:

When I undertook my crossword-solving self-improvement program in the early 1980s, I had no idea whether it was possible to, in effect, teach my brain to think better—to recall facts faster, to perceive wordplay more easily, to cast a wider net in thinking about possible meanings of words used in clues, and just generally sharpen my mental acuity. But clearly, with my drills and practice, I managed to accomplish a significant improvement in a matter of months. I sensed at the time that solving crosswords had a very practical effect on the nimbleness of the human mind. Thus, I was not so much surprised as delighted when studies emerged a few years ago indicating a concrete mental benefit from regularly solving crossword puzzles and performing other brain-stimulating games and activities. Actually, I was beyond delighted; I was ecstatic, because the studies were conducted with a very particular purpose in mind: to see if exercising the mind diminishes the likelihood of developing Alzheimer's disease or senile dementia. The answer was an emphatic yes.

Two studies were particularly striking. One, from researchers at Case Western University and published in the *Proceedings of the National Academy of Sciences* in 2001, showed that adults who pursued intellectually stimulating games and hobbies were 2.5 times less likely to develop Alzheimer's than those who didn't. In 2003, researchers at the Albert Einstein College of Medicine of Yeshiva University, in New York, reported in the *New England Journal of Medicine* on a 21-year study of 469 men and women, with similar results. Participants in the upper third of the cognitive-activity scale (doing crossword puzzles regularly, reading, playing a musical instrument, etc.) were 63 percent less likely to develop dementia than those in the lowest third. And the more crossword-solving the better: Working on the puzzles four days a week

instead of once a week decreased the dementia risk by 47 percent. (Subsequent studies have confirmed these sorts of findings.)

This was one of those "wow" moments. Crosswords aren't just fun and challenging (as anyone who does them knows), and they don't just *seem* like they're good for your brain (as I had long suspected); they're *actually good* for you. This news would be welcomed by anyone, but it couldn't have come at a better time for the baby boom generation, a gigantic 76-million-strong demographic rabbit passing through the country's population python. Boomers (and I'm part of that huge cohort born between 1946 and 1964) had been in a low-grade panic about Alzheimer's and senile dementia. Their anxieties were kindled by coping with their own aging parents as they reached their 70s and 80s, and seeing how unkind those years can be. Boomers being boomers, sponsors of the most youth-obsessed era in the nation's history, they had desperately embraced every anti-aging, anti-Alzheimer's tactic imaginable, from gobbling down gingko biloba to guzzling so-called smart drinks. But now, with the studies at Case Western, Albert Einstein College, and other universities, here was proof of a tangible way to give yourself a fighting chance at warding off, or at least substantially reducing, the risk of falling prey to old age's debilitating effects on the mind.

With the first baby boomers having just turned 60 in 2006 and their retirement years on the horizon, it's a fine thing that the crossword puzzle, though a 93-year-old codger itself, has been rejuvenated by technological innovations that make the puzzle constructor's job easier and the puzzles' availability—whether on a newspaper's Web site, a cell phone, or a handheld device—more widespread than Arthur Wynne could have ever imagined. But those developments aren't good enough. As an aspiring Arthur Wynne 2.0, I'd love to lead crosswords into a digital revival that keeps boomers, and their children and grandchildren, puzzle-enthralled well into their silver years.

CHAPTER FIVE

Pulling Back the Curtain: The Hidden Rules of the Grid

I've already passed along the general guidelines that govern the construction and solving of crossword puzzles, a roadmap that should help any solver reach the grid's end with few wrong turns. But then there are the hidden rules, the unspoken conventions and deep traditions that are the true engines of professional puzzle construction. Knowing them will not only make solving easier, it will (presumably) make the process a lot more fun. As you scan the clues, you'll be thinking like a crossword puzzle constructor—or at least thinking like one without mentally computing how many hours you put into making the puzzle versus the amount that you'll be paid for it and realizing that it would be more lucrative to work at Wendy's telling people "that'll-be-$7.43-pull-up-to-the-second-window." The hidden rules are the stuff no computer software could ever duplicate; they're the equivalent of a secret handshake that could save many a frustrated solver from hurling a half-completed Sunday puzzle across the room. Smartypants civilians figure out some, or most, of these rules on their own, after much trial and error, but there's no reason for the rest of the world to suffer. If trying to solve puzzles without knowing these rules is like traveling in a foreign country without knowing the language, then this chapter is a Berlitz course. Except you don't forget everything if you don't use it for a few weeks.

Now, crossword-puzzle editors all have their own idiosyncratic rules. But ever since the new-wave crossword revolution overthrew the Maleskacized method of puzzle-making, the new generation of editors tends to approach crosswords with a shared affection for puzzles that include an entertaining mix of humor, pop-culture references, lively word selection, and a pedantry-free familiarity with traditional areas of knowledge like literature, art, and geography. The preferences I'm passing along here apply to the puzzles I edit, but I'm confident in saying that they're generally applicable to most contemporary puzzles. (Well, my prohibition of sexual references and explicit language meshes with pretty much everyone else's. I am aware of an outfit, which shall remain nameless, that specializes in obscene crosswords. But don't get me started on that subject; dirty-word puzzles make me cross.)

It's essential to understand how constructors arrive at themes for their puzzles, because once you've discovered a puzzle's theme and are madly scribbling down the answers, it starts a cascade of solutions throughout the puzzle. For many solvers, the moment when a puzzle's theme reveals itself is a minor miracle, like a bit of magic where a thoroughly scissored dollar bill suddenly comes together into a whole. It can seem as if constructors tap almost any source for themes, but a fairly strict set of rules governs their selection. Knowing these rules in advance can save you from taking a stab at solving theme answers using an approach that, by definition, is fated not to work. For starters, a good crossword puzzle is not going to use theme answers that involve repetition of the same word (SEARS TOWER, EIFFEL TOWER, LEANING TOWER). Some editors allow this duplication—but like I said, a good puzzle won't use it, and I'm the arbiter of what's good in my little world. Filling in answers of the TOWER-TOWER-TOWER variety starts to feel like rote work instead of fun.

That's not to say that I ban any use of the same word more than once in a puzzle theme. But it's gotta show some spark. I recently received a puzzle submission that uses the word ANT over and over again in its theme and is going to be a terrific crossword. What, you might ask, is so interesting about using a humble three-letter word? In this case, the three letters are buried in each answer—and not only that, each answer is a city: MORGANTOWN, SAN ANTONIO, etc. It reminds me of a recent puzzle that has become a favorite of mine. It was entitled "Split Pea," but the theme had nothing to do with soup. The beginnings and endings of the theme answers were . . . well, you figure it out: PICNIC AREA, PETER FONDA, PERESTROIKA. I particularly liked this because the PEA was split in different ways, sometimes the P at the start, and the EA at the end, or a PE and then the A.

The "Split Pea" puzzle was made by Fred Piscop, the friend from my word-game group who went on to become the editor of the *Washington Post*'s Sunday puzzle. The other puzzle, with the hidden ANTs, was made by a constructor who's not going anywhere, as far as I know: He's an inmate of the Florida state penitentiary system. I can't put a number on it, but a healthy portion of crossword puzzles published in America are created by constructors who are "guests of the state," as the saying goes. It's not surprising, when you think about it. These guys have plenty of time on their hands, obviously, plus convicts are perhaps the only people around to whom the 50 bucks or so that they'd receive for their hours of labor actually looks like a handsome reward. When you're making eight cents an hour working in the prison machine shop, or whatever it is prisoners are paid, a double-digit check is a fortune.

Just as I ban word repetition in theme answers, I also reject puzzles that rely on rhyming answers because, well, they're just painfully insipid. It doesn't require much, or any, creativity to come up with rhyming words, and solving puzzles with rhyming answers is almost insulting. If you've solved the first two of three theme

answers that rhyme, filling out the third answer—*huh, it sounds just like the first two . . . imagine that*—makes solvers feel like they're back in kindergarten.

Just as theme answers try to avoid being too simplistic, they also avoid testing specialized areas of knowledge. So don't start scratching your head over a partially solved theme answer, thinking that it's seeking some obscure nugget of information you won't know. Maybe the folks at NFL.com are even now coming up with a theme puzzle involving the names of football coaches from the 1970s, but trust me, the puzzles in general-interest publications will not require you to know that Hank Stram coached the Kansas City Chiefs back then. And beware of suspecting that the theme (or, for that matter, any of the clues) is asking for specialized local or regional knowledge. It's not likely to, because contemporary constructors realize that there's no challenge in tricking a solver with a clue that requires an answer that's just going to make the solver shrug when it's revealed. I won't allow references to products that aren't distributed nationally, because, for instance, there's no reason why anyone in California should know that Hellmann's is a brand of mayonnaise; it's only sold east of the Rockies. Not that I need another reason to tell constructors to hold the mayo if it's Hellmann's, but I'd also nix it because using it would reinforce an old complaint about crosswords that they reflect a New York bias.

Many puzzle editors and constructors come from the Northeast, and the orientation of puzzles did (and does, sometimes) skew in that direction. All I know is that you won't find references to New York City subway lines in *my* puzzles.

Other no-nos:

- Any wit-free displays of flat-footed obviousness. I don't ever want to see another puzzle that involves colors or body parts, two themes that for some reason appeal to fledgling (and sometimes fledged) constructors. Maybe if you combined the two, with answers like GREEN THUMB, REDHEAD, WHITE KNUCKLES, etc., they would work, but otherwise: No thanks.

- Answers pegged to death, drugs, or disease. Constructors try to maintain a certain decorum, in general. You're not likely to see anything more serious than the FLU in a puzzle. CANCER is just an astrological sign in our world. And we've won the war on drugs: OPIUM is just a pricey fragrance. Will Shortz, I've noticed, likes to push the envelope in his puzzles, but that means nothing more daring than employing the answer SCHMUCKS.

- Unusual or obscure words. For all the reasons I've harped on earlier.

Constructors live in this realm between two force fields, the obscure and the obvious. Both are to be avoided. The temptation to stray into either one comes from a kind of weakness: You lapse into cluing LAMB with "Mary had a little ____" simply from a failure of imagination (and using poor old Charles Lamb to excuse the answer ELIA, his pseudonym, is another sort of triteness. Lamb is the Mel Ott of English essayists: famous in his day, but immortal in crosswords because of a happy arrangement of vowels and consonants). But using obscure words in a puzzle is another kind of crutch for the constructor: It stems either from a character flaw that delights in humiliating one's fellow human beings, and thus should not be indulged, or it comes from a late-night desperation to get out of a tricky patch of puzzle that's under construction and ESNE is the word of last resort. Most editors rarely allow ESNE-style words anymore, and longtime constructors who still want to sell their puzzles have to learn not to rely on them.

It might seem, from the solver's side of things, that constructors approach each individual clue afresh, trying to come up with a clever way of setting up the desired answer. And indeed constructors do always have an antenna up, looking for an opportunity to tickle themselves and solvers with a devilish hint. But it would be exhausting and horribly time-consuming to begin each puzzle from scratch. The truth is that there is an extensive array of clue types and clue devices that we rely on, a cluing toolbox that we use to build puzzles. When the opportunity presents itself to do something inspired and out of left field, that's wonderful. But the basic process of cluing involves drawing on these basic templates. For solvers, knowing what clue types are being used in a puzzle, and thus recognizing what sort of answer the constructor is going after, is the equivalent of a baseball player studying videotapes of opposing pitchers in order to figure out what pitches are coming in certain situations. Sometimes pitchers, through an inadvertent shoulder dip or chin tuck, tip off batters; here I'm going to do it on purpose. Don't worry, I'm not violating some sort of magicians' code, risking the ire of my peers by giving away professional secrets. Puzzle constructors want solvers to get as much fun and satisfaction as possible from crosswords. I think that familiarity with the clue types gives solvers a bit of an edge the next time they sit down to wrestle with a puzzle.

Let's start with the types of theme puzzles.

Inner clue: theme clues that seemingly have no relation to each other, until you see that a certain word within the answer has an unexpected commonality with words in other answers. Chew on these: SMART COOKIE, PIE IN THE SKY, CAKE OF SOAP, DANISH CITY.

Straight list: Admittedly, not the most inspired theme idea,

but nice for an early-in-the-week puzzle not meant to be too tricky. Clues for straight-list themes might call for synonyms for "goodbye," or titles of Dr. Seuss books, or kinds of Mexican food.

Quote or quip: A generally humorous line that breaks up symmetrically as it unfolds across the grid so that the theme answers fit nicely in the puzzle, as with:

ETIQUETTE IS
KNOWING HOW TO
YAWN WITH YOUR
MOUTH CLOSED

Credit for this one goes to constructor Doug Peterson, an accountant who lives in Pasadena, California. As Doug knows, the best of these quote/quips end with the punchline where it belongs, at the end.

Then there are all the non-theme clues and clue devices that constructors use. The most common, of course, would be the straight definition/synonym clue. "Possess": OWN, "Capital of Maine": AUGUSTA. But there are many, many others.

Example clues: These will offer a word, followed by "or," "and," "e.g.," "for one," or "for example," which signal that the constructor wants you to go from the specificity of the clue to an answer that is more general. "Sycamore or chestnut": TREE,

"Sculpture, e.g.": ART. (If I want to make the latter clue a tad more difficult, I'll say "Sculptures," which might seem to be fishing for a plural answer ending in "s.")

Foreign words: Without getting too recherché about it, commonly understood words from other languages can spice up the grid. "House, to Hernando": CASA, "French friend": AMI.

Abbreviations: Either the clue itself will contain an abbreviation, tipping off the solver that the answer also will be an abbreviation ("Col.'s boss": GEN), or the clue will be followed by "Abbr." ("Civil War side: Abbr.": CSA).

Comparatives/superlatives: "More sensible": SANER, for example, or "Most sensible": SANEST.

Fill-in-the-blanks (and parentheticals): Both types of clues are firing blanks at the solver. One is straightforward and self-explanatory: "Gone With the ____": WIND. The other provides a blank-equipped phrase, followed by a parenthetical bit of explanation. "From ___ Z (completely)": A TO.

Referentials: These send the solver on a little treasure hunt in the puzzle. The clue for 10 Across might be "With 56 Across, *M*A*S*H* star": ALAN, and 56 Across is just "See 10 Across": ALDA. And by the way, if any of you aspiring actors out there are thinking of changing your name, intend to become famous, and would love to see your name frequently in crossword puzzles long after your celebrity has cooled off, choose something that's short—say, about four letters, with as many vowels as possible. Constructors have just about worn out Mr. Alda's name. We were practically dancing in the streets in 1988 when the song "Orinoco Flow" became a hit—not because the music was so wonderful, which it might very well be, but because it signaled the arrival of the singer ENYA. That's four letters, with two-and-a-half of them vowels. She joined the crossword pantheon, going up alongside AIDA, ARES, and Mr. Alda. I should note here that constructors like referentials a lot more than solvers do; one of the more common complaints I hear from solvers is that they find it really, really annoying to have to go searching for 56 Across when they're working on 10 Across. But, well, constructors like using every tool in the box.

Slang terms/colloquial phrases: Sometimes explicitly tagged as such ("slangily," "so to speak"), as with "Attorney, slangily": MOUTHPIECE, or "Peek, so to speak": GANDER. Then again, sometimes there's no tag signaling that something slangy is required: "Leave in a hurry": LAM IT.

Evocatives: These cleverly paint a word picture and occasionally feel—dare I say it?—almost like a bit of poetry. Or at least doggerel. "Bachelor's last words": I DO, for instance, or "Bathwater tester": TOE.

Name clues: Generally, these offer a title of a book or movie or some other well-known work, followed by the word "name." Greta Garbo might have wanted to be left alone, but if pesky crossword constructors are in need of a double-consonant-vowel-consonant-vowel solution, they'll often go with "*Ninotchka* name": GRETA. (Actually, constructors don't call the stuff that you write into the grid "solutions," or even "answers." We call it "fill," which to my ear has an unfortunate, slightly pejorative sound, like garbage going into a landfill, but there you are.)

Portionals: Clues that begin with the phrase "Part of" or "Half of," and can be meant literally or figuratively. "Part of a shirt": POCKET, or "Part of NATO": NORTH, or "Half of AD": ANNO. I like this last one, because for a half-second "AD" might make the solver think the clue is referring to an advertisement. Even when it's inadvertent and fleeting, constructors love anything that distracts or disorients solvers—and, of course, solvers like it too, because that's a substantial part of the fun of working on crosswords: blundering down wrong turns and experiencing that eureka moment when the correct path is revealed.

Hedgers: Sounds like shrubbery-oriented clues, but they're the ones that include "maybe," "sometimes," "at times," "often," or "usually." A couple of classics: "Farmer, at times": HOER, and "Penny, perhaps": ANTE.

X, to Y clues: These refer to relationships that can be adversarial

("Bluto, to Popeye": FOE) or familial ("Judy, to Liza": MOM). Of course, some folks might think that the familial is by definition adversarial, but I'll leave that to a shrink to sort out.

Inherent hints: A word in the clue tips off a particular way it should be answered. The clue "Oscar role for Julia" could be read several ways: Did Raul Julia ever play Mr. Madison in *The Odd Couple*? Or did he win an Academy Award for something else? Or maybe it's referring to an actress—Julia, Julia . . . Julia Roberts? What did she win an Oscar for? Oh, yes, that blowsy self-taught lawyer, whatshername, Erin Go Braless, no, no, Erin Brockovich. Yes, that's it! *Erin Brockovich.* Now, what was that clue again? "Oscar role for Julia." Hmm, the grid says the answer's four letters . . . must be ERIN. And, yes, that's correct. But, then, if the solver recognized that this was an "inherent" clue, the fact that it employed just the actress's first name meant that the answer would mirror it, needing just the character's first name as well. [Note: About that "braless" jest: I'd never make a slightly risqué joke like that in my puzzles, so I thought I'd get it off my chest here.]

Colloquials: They're of the fill-in-the-blank variety, but want the solver to provide the rest of a commonly spoken phrase: "What's ____ for me?": IN IT.

Nicknames: "Mr. Television": BERLE.

Likers: Clues that start with the word "like" and are fishing for adjectival answers. "Like Santa Claus": OBESE, or "Like some loose-leaf paper": LINED.

Roman numerals: Though it may seem like the only time you see Roman numerals anymore is in association with the Super Bowl (and I wonder how many people saw the name of the 2006 incarnation and thought Super Bowl XL would be followed in 2007 by the even bigger Super Bowl XXL), they still have a home in crossword puzzles. Often the clues using them are rendered as a math problem: "One-tenth of MDX": CLI.

"It" or "They" starters: Beware, clues that begin with "It" or "They" are often signaling that they're going for something tricky. "It won't hold water": SIEVE.

Kinships: These use "kin" or "relative" to signal a taxonomic or functional closeness, not actual familial ties. "Oyster kin": CLAM, or "Button relative": VELCRO.

Antonyms: Just simple clues asking for opposites. "Not hard": EASY. In more ways than one.

"Brieflys" and "for-shorts": Sometimes constructors are asking for shortened forms of words, or even abbreviations, but don't want to go the "abbr." route if they've already used that form in a puzzle. The shortened form might be clued "Physician, for short": DOC, and the non-"abbr." abbreviation could be "Nest egg, for short": IRA. Occasionally the clue will ask for "letters," which is another way of getting at "abbr." without using that again ("Space shuttle letters": NASA).

"X, as Y": This form is asking for what amounts to a "partial synonym," words that add up to the same thing within a specific context. "Improve, as wine": AGE.

Archaics: When you see a clue that includes the phrase "Old-style" or the word "once," it's looking for the archaic or obsolete form of a word. "Formerly, old-style": ERST. (Maybe that clue should read "olde-style"?)

Starters-enders/Beginners-enders: Whatever you call them, they're clues looking for prefixes or suffixes. "Nautical starter": AERO, for instance, or "Ending for press": URE. Both of these are nice because, unless you're wise in the ways of construction, it's not immediately apparent where the clues are going. "Nautical starter"—the solver might panic for moment, thinking the puzzle wants the term used for the ignition system on a cruise ship, or wondering if there's some salty-dog phrase for the person who signals the beginning of a regatta. And "Ending for press" could send the solver into thoughts about a printing press running out of ink or something similarly mistaken. But if you know that "starter" and "ending" are code for prefix and suffix, then the press-ure is off.

Wordplay variations: I admit it, coming up with this kind of clue tickles me to no end—because it makes the constructor feel rather witty for a moment or two, but also because you know you're embedding a clue in a puzzle that the solver is going to smile over when the answer becomes apparent. "Kitchen extension" just sounds good, for starters, plus it conjures visions of a trip to Home Depot. But the answer is actually a branch of the starter-ender category: ETTE. "Introduction to physics" might produce a mild groan in the solver, or set off thoughts of apples dropping on Newton's head. It's a nice moment when the answer is unveiled: META.

Plurals: Any clue given as a plural requires a plural answer, and sometimes the constructor goes fishing for them. I might find a spot in a puzzle that works with fill that spells out GEORGES; instead of casting around for other combinations of crossing words that would allow me to put something else in that space, I forge ahead, cluing it with "Bush namesakes"—which has the advantage, because all clues start with a capital letter, of potentially tripping up the solver momentarily by raising the possibility that I'm asking for the namesakes of a kind of vegetation. Roses? Rhododendrons? If the solver gets the crossing letter G to start things off, or just thinks on the clue for an extra moment, the correct path should become apparent.

Rivals, competitors, alternatives: Generally, this is a hint that the constructor is looking for that long-ago taboo of the crossword world, the brand name. "Avis alternative": HERTZ, or "Paper Mate competitor": BIC.

Prepositional additionals: A shorthand way of making a clue/answer work. "Depend (on)": RELY or "Got hip, with 'up'": WISED.

Ellipses: Just like a writer quoting a phrase found elsewhere, but not a complete thought, a crossword constructor needs to signal the reader that only a fragment is under consideration. Hamlet's soliloquy starts out beautifully, of course: "To be, or not to be: that is the question:/ Whether 'tis nobler in the mind to suffer/ The slings and arrows of outrageous fortune,/ Or to take arms against a sea of troubles,/And by opposing end them?" But it's a tad long for crossword-puzzle cluing purposes. Especially if I just need to clue the four-letter fill OR TO. Unlike the fence-sitting Prince of Denmark, I wouldn't hesitate to clue it "____ take arms . . . "

Location, location, location: The use of the word "home" or "site" in a clue means the constructor is looking for either a literal or figurative place. And it often presents an inviting opportunity for bit of misdirection. A four-letter answer for "Hatchling's home" might be NEST, but it could also be TREE. Just as "Columbus' home" could prompt solvers to start thinking, "Hmm, Columbus was Italian, wasn't he? But didn't he live in Spain?" Instead of just jotting down the answer: OHIO.

Partnerships: This is another way of cluing that calls for either literal or figurative answers. When the constructor throws the word "partner" (or "colleague") into a clue, it could mean an actual associate, as with "Currier's partner": IVES, or just a word that is almost joined at the hip with another in a common phrase: "Bill's partner"—*no, not Hillary*, it's COO. (Which reminds me, it seems like I'm seeing more and more corporate executives referred to as the Chief Operating Officer or COO; maybe I need to work up an abbr. clue for that one.)

Concerns/banes: Evocative clues that make the solver daydream for a moment about what the clue suggests (I believe that this type of clue was originated by Will Weng at the *Times*). "Golfer's concern" briefly sends the solver out onto the course, to ponder all the things that could require a golfer's attention: If it's a three-letter answer, maybe it's the LIE of the fairway shot he faces. Four letters: his GRIP on the club. Five: SCORE. Or maybe it's a big ol' six-letter solution: STANCE. The clue "Librarian's bane" transports the solver into the stacks to imagine what annoys a librarian. An overdue book? One shelved in the wrong place? But the answer, my friend, is blowing loudly and repeatedly like a Canadian goose into a Kleenex or talking on a cell phone: NOISE.

The Exes: Constructors use "onetime" or "former" to elicit answers that capture situations or relationships that are no longer operative. "Former UN member" not only signals that the constructor is looking for an ex-member of that organization, but also one that, like "UN," employs initials. Hence: USSR.

Last, and possibly least, because they occur so infrequently but remain plenty devious, are the **Basic Confusables:** These are the pies in the face, the trapdoors, the whoopee cushions of crosswords. And the amazing thing is that they're just happenstance—they crop up as a result of solvers running countless possibilities for solutions through their minds, rather than constructors sifting the entire language for certain quirks. Confronted with the clue "Prohibit" for a three-letter answer that already has been filled in with B-A by letters from crossing words, many solvers will be tempted to quickly scribble down an "N" to finish the answer. But the constructor might actually be looking for BAR.

Basic Confusables come in a variety of forms—as verbs, nouns, place names, actors' names, mythology, and many others. In almost any realm of language, there can exist a useful pair of words that share certain letters and plausibly might be the answer for the same clue. What's the four-letter first name that answers "Actress ____ Thompson"? Fans of the movies *Love, Actually* and *Sense and Sensibility* might be inclined to jot down the answer EMMA; they wouldn't love it, actually, if they later learned that the constructor's sense and sensibility leaned more toward the 1970s TV series *Family* and the actress who played the mom in that show: SADA Thompson. (This one will be particularly irksome if the solver happens to get a crossing word that first offers up the fourth letter, A.)

Oh, the unforeseen possibilities of Basic Confusables in the grid are endless. Quick, a German river, four letters, with the last letter an "R"—would that be the SAAR or the RUHR? An old French coin ending in "U," three letters: If you made the obvious and completely understandable choice, SOU, that answer wouldn't be worth a plugged nickel if the constructor wanted the less commonly known ECU. What about a Greek god whose name has four letters, the second of which is "R" and the fourth of which is "S"? Certainly ARES presents himself as a likely answer. But if you've got your mind in the gutter, you'll find EROS. (The only reason why crossword constructors don't make a point of using Basic Confusables is that we can't predict the order in which solvers will fill in answers—the old BAR/BAN wheeze doesn't work if the solver happened to come up with a crossing solution that produced the R or the N before the BA.)

So there you have it: The Rosetta _____ of the cluing arts. Becoming intimately familiar with these types of clues—to the point where you almost instantly recognize which type of clue is being employed from the moment you clap eyes on it when you're working on a puzzle—should make your solving move along much more smoothly. But be warned: A well-edited puzzle will use many of the cluing varieties listed above, and most editors will try not to repeat their use in the same puzzle. Still, I suspect that knowing these strategies will increase your confidence, because becoming

familiar with the constructor's playbook means you're competing on a more level playing field.

But don't get cocky. There are still a few nuances of the grid left to be revealed.

CHAPTER SIX

Master Class: Getting Tournament-Ready (or at Least Saturday-Savvy)

I've had a front-row seat in the crossword business for more than two decades, and over that time I've noticed that elite solvers—the ones who consistently finish high on the tournament level or who are just demons on an everyday, non-competitive level—share certain attributes. As someone who also had the experience of designing a crash course in crossword mastery that enabled me to become a national crossword champion, I also know that these qualities can be nurtured and developed by folks who would like to raise their crossword skills to tournament level—or at least to the point where a Saturday Stumper leaves them largely unstumped. Herewith, then:

The Five Championship-Clinching Traits of the Gridmasters

1. A Robust, Wide-Ranging, Malleable, and Ever-Growing Vocabulary

When the average American adult is having a conversation, the words that he or she uses are generally drawn from a base of about 3,000—unless that conversation is taking place in the form of e-mail, in which case the store of words employed is probably about, oh, 175, most of them misspelled. (The average American teenager, of course, no longer has a vocabulary and instead communicates exclusively with abbreviations and initials via instant messages sent to someone just across the room. Please note that this parenthetical comment is about to end with an actual period and closed parenthesis—I am not attempting, through the use of an "emoticon," to use typography to simulate the appearance of a one-eyed grinning fool.)

Our conversational vocabulary of 3,000 words represents less than one-sixth of the total words with which we're familiar; most of us actually know and recognize about 20,000 words. That national average may drop substantially when William F. Buckley finally shuffles off this mortal coil (that phrase is from a certain play about a Danish prince, ______), but there's no reason why we should rely on the estimable Mr. Buckley to prop up our stats. In fact, there's a very good reason why we should do everything in our power to begin increasing our store of words *right now*—and it doesn't have anything to do with those late-night TV ads and radio commercials promising that building a better vocabulary will win you promotion after promotion at work and make you irresistible to the opposite sex. Nice as those benefits might be, they're nothing compared with the ultimate reward: better grid performance.

As you might expect from a former bond analyst and co-author of *The Million Word Crossword Dictionary,* I am wont to view crosswords through a statistical lens. It turns out that fully half of all the answers in crossword puzzles are drawn from a pool of about 5,000 words of three, four, or five letters in length. Five thousand short, simple words—a quarter of the average American vocabulary—will provide 50 percent of the answers to most puzzles. The room for creativity lies in the other half of crossword vocabulary, and that's why it's vital to keep expanding your own store of words if you're going to elevate your puzzle abilities to the expert realm. That creative half of the answers might or might not overlap with the other 15,000 words in the average vocabulary that don't fall into the easy, three-to-five-letter category.

As you might also expect, my previous career on Wall Street was not exactly a fount of new vocabulary words—at least not ones that weren't worthy of an R rating. (Here's the only G-rated joke I ever heard during my Wall Street days: What's the difference between a bond and a bond trader? Bonds mature.) And by the way, isn't it quaint that Hollywood still bothers to rate its movies when in the past decade we've somehow become the filthiest-mouthed nation on the planet? Another attractive quality of crossword puzzles: Their

four-letter words aren't four-letter words. If anything, my vocabulary likely would have atrophied over the years if I hadn't embarked on my crossword self-improvement campaign in the early 1980s and then continued to build my vocabulary even after I achieved my goals at national tournaments. My policy of looking up every unfamiliar word I encountered—whether it was in a difficult puzzle, a book, or a newspaper article—became a habit that not only made me a better crossword solver and constructor, but also simply increased my enjoyment of language and conversation.

So by all means, look up any unfamiliar words you come across in the course of a day, but don't just look 'em up and consider your duty done. It helps immensely to write down the words and their definitions—neurological studies indicate that the act of physically writing out a piece of information strengthens the web of neuron connections in the brain associated with the info, making it more readily accessible in your memory banks. It doesn't take a very complicated math calculation to figure out that if you make one notation per day regarding a strange word, after three years you'll have added more than a thousand words to your vocabulary.

Please don't talk yourself out of trying this approach by assuming that since there's no way of knowing whether the new words you learn will ever actually crop up in a crossword, there's no point to the exercise. Trust me, they will. Sorry to be such a bore by harking back to my tournament victories, but I can attest that, between my first entry into a crossword tourney and my wins a year later, new words that I had added to my collection of notecards absolutely appeared in the championship puzzles and I gleefully zipped right through them. Diligence rewarded is a delightful experience.

Back then, I was looking up words in an old-fashioned, paper-and-glue, honest-to-God dictionary. That used to be a disincentive to check the definitions of words: the chore of getting up and hoisting a dictionary. These days, with dictionaries built into word-processing programs and available for free online, there's hardly any excuse not to quickly check the definition of every exotic (or just sorta interesting) word you come across. And don't just glance at the first definition and be done with it; take a moment to understand the origin of the word, and to let its various other meanings sink in. In difficult puzzles, constructors may well use second or third definitions of relatively commonplace words. The clue "Conveyance requirement" might prompt you to start thinking that the four-letter solution has something to do with a vehicle used as a form of conveyance—maybe a TIRE? No, unless we're talking about a unicycle, it would be "requirements," plural, and TIRES. Uh, okay, then how about . . . ROAD? Wait a second. There's another definition of "conveyance," which describes the word as a legal term for a transfer of property. "Conveyance requirement," then, could very well be a DEED.

The general policy among contemporary crossword editors is not to employ obscure words simply to lord them over mystified solvers. The practice used to be much more common and seemed to have the sole purpose of bestowing an air of erudition on the constructor—one that was completely illegitimate, of course, because anyone can ransack a dictionary for little-known words. Their appearance in a puzzle doesn't mean that the constructor had ever heard of them before putting them to use. I sincerely doubt that Eugene Maleska's vocabulary included the word "battologize" (meaning "to keep repeating needlessly") before he began editing the *Times* puzzle, yet it was a frequent guest in his puzzles—which, I guess, means he battologized "battologize."

I'm hardly an enemy of using unusual, interesting words in puzzles. It's just that I believe that the words should have some useful, real-world context (a belief now commonplace in the puzzle business). It doesn't hurt if they're also ripe for use in an amusing play on words. "Maker of batteries" sounds like an innocuous enough clue for a nine-letter answer. EVEREADY? Oops, that's eight letters. DURACELL? Ouch, that's eight letters, too. Maybe this isn't going to be as easy as it seems. Ah, my friend, I hate to break it to you, but there's some puzzle trickery at work here. A "batterie" happens to be a term in ballet for any action in which the dancer's legs beat together, usually in mid-air. So a nine-letter "Maker of batteries" is a BALLERINA. Which brings us to . . .

2. A Knowledge Base That's as Broad as the Mississippi River (One Mile at Its Widest, Just Below the Confluence With the Missouri)

I am not someone whom you'll ever hear leaving Lincoln Center after a performance of *Swan Lake*, sighing and saying dreamily, "I love the dance." Ballet just isn't something that ever appealed to me, not as a kid growing up in Brooklyn or as an adult working on Wall Street. Just wasn't on my cultural menu. Yet I know what a "batterie" is because I realized that ballet terminology was a gap in my knowledge base, and if I was going to become an expert solver I'd need to be able to readily answer clues on the subject—rather than, as was the case before my self-education campaign began, solving ballet-related clues by relying on crossing words to reveal the answer.

The best thing about ballet, in the mind of this philistine, is that—if you're lucky—there's no singing involved. This makes ballet infinitely superior to opera, for which I have an even more intense allergy. Somebody once said that going to the opera is like going on a plane trip when you're afraid of flying: You're trapped for hours on end in a cramped seat, and you get the terrible feeling that before long somebody's going to die. That's a night at the opera, in my mind, which is why I'd much rather stay home and watch Groucho, Harpo, and Co. in *A Night at the Opera*. Friends used to invite me to go to the opera with them, and my standard reply was,

"Great—as long as there's no singing in a foreign language." They don't ask anymore.

And yet, despite my ignorant attitude toward the subject, I'm not in fact an opera ignoramus. As with ballet, I realized that my lack of familiarity with the opera world was a weak spot in my solving game. Opera references kept coming up in puzzles, and I would simply draw a blank that stayed as blank as the grid where the answer was supposed to go until I could deploy the letters from crossing words to give me the answer. This had to stop, so I decided to study opera. Or, rather, to study *about* opera—I wasn't interested in learning the art of hysterical bellowing. And now I'm reasonably well versed in the subject. Giuseppe Verdi? Even before my home-schooling sessions, I knew that he wrote *Aïda*—that's a crossword war-horse, because its three-out-of-four vowels make it the opera most beloved by puzzle constructors. But now I know much more about Verdi—other major works, of course, such as *Rigoletto, La Traviata*, and *Otello* (no h!), but also his lesser-known operas, such as *Ernani,* based on the play *Hernani* by Victor ugo—sorry—Hugo.

Sadly, I couldn't hum a bar from any of these operas. Maybe in another life I'll be more esthetically sensitive. But in this one, I can at least power through opera-related crossword puzzle clues—and take no small pleasure in the realization that I have added a new area of learning to my store of knowledge. There's something depressing, as an adult, about realizing how much of the information you crammed into your head in high school and college has gradually leached out of your skull and into the ether, never to be rattled off to a demanding teacher again. Revolutionary War generals, botanical terminology, whole areas of calculus, the name of that cute girl in the third row—all are part of a vanished world. One of the delights of my resolution to become better at crosswords was the sense that I was fighting this withering-away of my memory banks.

It's easy, almost compulsory, for adults to slip into mental ruts, on the job and at home, where only certain areas of knowledge are required. The rest is optional. Of course, some self-starters never stop learning throughout adult life, eagerly taking up new subjects or diving deeper and deeper into realms of learning that they already love. But plenty of folks aren't quite so "proactive." (Don't you hate it when you find yourself using buzzwords that you detest? I usually want to proactively kick in the shin anyone who uses that word, and yet there it is.) So, then, let the urge to improve your crossword-solving ability provide the impetus to start taking up unfamiliar subjects. In doing so, of course, it would help if you share another trait that is common among crossword champs:

3. An Insatiable, Thoroughgoing, Relentless, Cat-Shaming Curiosity

A yearning to find out stuff is the engine that drives the previous two entries. You can will yourself to be the sort of person who instantly turns to the dictionary to look up unfamiliar words, or consults an encyclopedia (or Google) upon encountering a reference to the Potsdam Conference but can't quite remember who was doing the conferring or why (Stalin, Truman, Churchill and, after Winston was ousted as prime minister in 1945, Clement Attlee; they met near Berlin to make arrangements to start the Cold War, er, make agreements regarding the post-war era). But it helps if, instead of approaching this sort of amateur research as a chore, you bring to it an avidness for the hunt, a.k.a. curiosity.

By all means, constantly monitor what you read or hear on the radio or television for unfamiliar words or facts. But also try to vary your reading habits—if you're a World War II buff who knows the Potsdam Conference down to the seating arrangements, but you continue to grab any new book about the war that comes out, or habitually watch the History Channel for its latest exploration of the subject, that's not so much indulging your curiosity as tossing yourself intellectual softballs. Break out into other areas where your knowledge base is thin—your brain will thank you, of course, but the effort will almost certainly be rewarded somewhere down the line by a seemingly impossible crossword clue that happens to tap a subject that you've studied. And this doesn't necessarily mean becoming well versed in the methodology of medieval manuscript illumination; it can also mean going beyond your mastery of 1970s TV trivia—no one can *touch* you on the subject of *Welcome Back,*

Kotter—and learning about, say, Ernie Kovacs' amazing TV comedy work in the 1950s and early 1960s.

The essential thing is to develop a heightened hunger for information in general. At first you'll likely start poking around on the edges of topics that you already know something about, but before long, you'll find yourself inquiring into realms of knowledge you might never have predicted would be of interest. Like opera.

I know, I know: It sounds a lot like the homework drudgery of junior high school, but all I can say is that the pleasure of acing a Saturday Stumper puzzle far exceeds any thrill you might have gotten from doing well on a long-forgotten social studies quiz. But on a more important level (and let's pretend here for a moment that there is something in life more important than crossword puzzles), fostering a sense of curiosity about the world and adopting a thirsty attitude toward learning are grand human impulses. Alas, they're also easy to neglect as the years go by, even though they have lasting benefits—not just because they'll heighten your own sense of enjoyment and understanding of the world, but because they're just plain old good for you (remember the section about Alzheimer's in Chapter Four?).

4. Flexibility (No Yoga Mat Required)

The first three traits I've mentioned have more to do with arming yourself before going to war with crosswords (girding for the

grid?). Mental flexibility, while certainly a quality that's essential in broadening your knowledge base or ramping up curiosity levels, is something I think of as characteristic of a crossword champ in the context of actual puzzle-solving. Mental flexibility is what enables the best solvers to sort out Basic Confusables (see Chapter Five) with little consternation. Like going to the gym with the intention of improving your physical flexibility, you could conceivably accomplish something on your own, but it's a heck of a lot easier to do it if you've got a personal trainer. Well, I'm here to be your mental-flexibility coach, and the best way I know to help others in this area is simply to demonstrate all the different bendy ways that crossword clues can be twisted. Follow along (you don't need to consult a physician before undertaking this program).

Grab the words in a clue and pull them apart to see if their surface meaning is what's under discussion, or if they're hiding what the constructor's really after. "Crete and Greece have one" (five letters) would appear to be testing your geographical knowledge. RIVER? Seems too generic. Something more Greekish is needed. You start rummaging around ancient gods, temples, Greek city names, etc. (Hey, ZORBA has five letters! Nah . . .). But then, if you just stretch your mind over the clue and reconsider it, maybe you don't need a Michelin guide at all in order to solve this one. What do "Crete" and "Greece" themselves share in common *as words*, rather than as places? Ah, yes: a LONG E.

Now get a grip on the clue "Champion rider." Study it closely. "Champion"—we all know what that means. "Rider"—now, if you're alive to possible uncommon usages of words in clues, you'll twig to the possibility that a "rider" can refer to a stipulation in a contract. But that's unlikely here—hard to see how it would work with "Champion." Hmmm, "Champion rider" . . . possibly a very successful jockey? ARCARO? No, not enough letters. The grid says we need a nine-letter answer. SHOEMAKER? No, that doesn't fit, because a crossing word tells us the first letter is G. Now bring the clue closer to your face . . . hold it . . . count to ten . . . think about it . . . be flexible . . . a-ha! "Champion" might not be a word describing the rider, it could be the name of a horse being ridden. Now, let's see, ROY ROGERS' horse was Trigger. Who's another cowboy star, starts with G, nine letters . . . GENE AUTRY!

And so it goes. The more flexible you are in reading clues, the more often you'll be rewarded with correct answers—and the more you'll begin to understand all the subterfuges and feints and misdirections employed by puzzle constructors. Like a stiff-as-a-board new arrival at the gym, who can barely manage a sit-up on day one and is slithering around doing yoga moves a few months later, you'll find that your increasing flexibility allows you to stretch in ways you never would have imagined as one successful pulling-apart of a crossword clue leads to another. At a certain point, you'll become a sort of crossword Gumby, unfazed by even the most devious puzzle

trickeration (Don King has a decidedly mixed record as a boxing promoter, but God bless him for inventing that word.).

"Sight from the Missouri" might send some solvers into silent contemplation of what might be seen from the Missouri River—Bluffs? St. Joseph? The mile-wide Mississippi just below the rivers' confluence?—but the flexy solver will note the italicized word in the clue and suss out that it refers to the battleship *Missouri*, which is part of the World War II memorial at PEARL HARBOR.

"Leaves home"—the flexy mind immediately challenges "Leaves" as to whether it's a verb or plural noun. If a verb, then the clue might head in the direction of DEPARTS or RUNS AWAY. But that's an awfully literal reading of the clue, which ought to set off your trickeration alarm. What would a more subtle reading of the clue conjure? Flip the clue around: What is a home for leaves? TREE.

"Steals"—verb or plural noun? If the latter, then it's likely the baseball STAT.

"They're not talking"—could be a divorcing couple, labor and management in a union dispute, or maybe prisoners refusing to answer questions. But these answers all have some sort of negative element, and tend in the direction that the constructor appears a little obviously to be trying to tempt you to go. The flexy mind considers the possibility that there's a positive angle, that "they" are quite happily "not talking." Then the answer would be MIMES (and who among us wouldn't prefer to see mimes helpfully completing a crossword grid rather than pretending to be stuck in a box?).

The essential thing about improving your mental flexibility as a tool for crossword success is never taking any clue in a difficult puzzle at face value. Be skeptical, ponder every new development from a variety of angles, assume that your opponent (the constructor) has evil intentions, and always, always keep your sense of humor at the ready. That's an excellent approach to solving crossword puzzles—and, come to think of it, not a bad one for getting through life.

5. Battle-Hardened, Puzzle-Toughened Experience, a.k.a. True Grid

If you're like many average crossword solvers, your solving routine probably is fairly predictable. You get the daily paper, which likely carries a syndicated puzzle that honors the usual Monday–Saturday build-up in difficulty. (I liken this arrangement to the *Jeopardy!* answer board on TV: If the subject is "Cities in England," you know that the most obvious solution, "Alex, what is London?," is very likely to be prompted by a hint in the cheapie top-of-the-board slot, and very *unlikely* to have anything to do with the more valuable bottom-of-the-board entries. With crosswords, you can almost be certain that there will be no tricky clues and answers on Monday, and you can be equally certain that on Saturday

almost all of them will be hard.) Some days, when you have time, you tackle the puzzle, and some days you don't. If the days when you have the time happen to fall early in the week, then you move smartly through the puzzle to completion with little trouble and a mild sense of accomplishment. If you're solving on a Friday, and have plenty of time, you get through with a good deal more difficulty, and a much bigger bump in pleasure when you fill in the last remaining answer square. If you have time on Saturday, amid all the chores and errands and other activities that eat up weekend hours, you might have a go at the Saturday puzzle, but with no expectation that you'll actually finish it—maybe yes, maybe no, depends on whether a sufficient number of wickedly difficult clues happen to be in areas of knowledge with which you're familiar.

This sort of catch-as-catch-can approach to crosswords is perfectly understandable. But it also ensures that whatever your crossword skill level is at this moment, that's what it's going to be five years from now. If you're intent on actually raising your solving ability, and thus maximizing the fun and enjoyment crosswords offer, then you're going to need to make a more concerted effort to consciously challenge yourself in an organized way.

The first step is to start solving puzzles from a variety of sources. The editor of your syndicated puzzle has a certain sensibility, one that your solving becomes attuned to. Despite editors' good-faith efforts at mixing things up and trying fresh approaches, the truth is that they often (and understandably) come up with clues that follow predictable patterns, draw on a familiar store of knowledge, and make jokes or plays on words that necessarily reflect a specific sense of humor. There will be some variety, based on who the constructor is, but the editor exercises a strong influence over tone and content. Your job is to break out of this crossword groove and start working on puzzles from other constructors and editors. If your daily puzzle isn't from the *New York Times*, start picking up that paper when you're pulling into 7-Eleven for a Slurpee or hitting Starbucks for a venti whatever. Will Shortz has done a superlative job at the *Times* for more than a decade. Even though that's a major accomplishment, Will's importance to crosswords hardly ends there. He's a wonderful ambassador for us, from his continuing to organize the big tournament in Stamford every year to his weekly word games on National Public Radio on Sunday mornings. Given the moribund state of the *Times* puzzle at the end of Maleska's reign, I hate to think where the popularity of crosswords might be today if Will hadn't taken over and injected such a fresh and inspired intelligence into what is still the most important and influential puzzle in the country. He single-handedly revitalized the *Times* crossword. Okay, he had some help from his constructors—the ones he brought on board, anyway, and maybe some of the Maleska holdovers (others had to learn a new way of cluing or find another place for their puzzles). Almost instantly upon becoming the editor of the *Times* puzzle, Will

doubled the fees paid for puzzles (Maleska always told constructors that, to his regret, he wasn't allowed to pay more for puzzles), and Will started attaching bylines to the crosswords, a welcome token of respect for constructors, of course, but also a sign that individual creativity and inventiveness were going to be rewarded.

Terrific as the Shortz-edited puzzles at the *Times* might be, if you are a regular *Times* solver, then you still need to branch out. You'll benefit from becoming familiar with a wide range of puzzles. Here are my favorite non-*Times*ian crosswords. Some can be found for free on the Internet, but others will cost a bit for access; all are invaluable.

- Mike Shenk's crossword in the Weekend section of the *Wall Street Journal* on Fridays. Out of the triumvirate of Mike Shenk, Merl Reagle, and Henry Hook that I idolized when I first got into the crossword world, only Mike has gone on to become a puzzle editor (Merl and Henry are still masterful puzzle constructors—see below). Mike was Will Shortz's assistant at *Games* magazine way back when, and even then he showed the sort of imagination and mathematical precision in his puzzle-making that helps make his *Journal* puzzle so appealing.
- Merl Reagle's Sunday puzzle in the *San Francisco Chronicle*—and in countless publications across the land. Merl is a demon at self-syndicating. I

used to think I was pretty good when I was doing it, but Merl is indefatigable about visiting papers himself and pitching his puzzle. And who can resist? I've always thought of Merl as operating in a parallel universe from the rest of us; he just sees connections and wordplay possibilities that don't occur to anyone else—except to his solvers, once they're enjoying the pleasure of solving one of Merl's hugely entertaining crosswords.

- Henry Hook's crosswords in the Sunday *Boston Globe* (alternating with the quite different but equally excellent puzzles constructed by Emily Cox and Henry Rathvon). As I said, Henry was one of the superstar puzzle constructors I most wanted to emulate when I began competing in tournaments. I've always thought of him as the sort of Groucho Marx of the crossword business; he's a fantastically nimble thinker, quick with the wisecracks and a master of the artful put-down, and there's a bit of his genius evident in every puzzle he constructs.

It's not just a matter of solving *more* puzzles, it's also a matter of solving *harder* puzzles, and gradually increasing the difficulty level of the crosswords you tackle as time passes. Sticking with the Monday-to-Saturday escalation of the challenge in your daily paper's crossword—without missing any days—is a good way to ensure that you're not slipping into the habit of tossing yourself softballs, working on only the puzzles that won't challenge you. If you think the early-in-the-week puzzles are so easy that you can't be bothered, I say: *not so fast.* Top-flight solvers have a secret technique for increasing the difficulty of any puzzle—a move that is kind of scary the first time you see it in action. Simply tear out the Across clues and *throw them away,* using only the Down clues to solve the puzzle. Suddenly, that piece-o'-cake Monday puzzle looks a tad harder, no?

Another way of using even easy puzzles to increase your effectiveness: Start timing yourself on them. Go for speed, but also accuracy. It will teach you how fast you can go without introducing errors into the grid, so that when your skills improve and you're able to breeze through a Friday or Saturday puzzle, you'll have a sense of what your fastest, yet still reliable, solving pace should be. Then work your way up over a matter of weeks or months. After a year, you'll be startled by the improvement in your game. I know that sounds like a long time, but consider: You will have acquired an ability that will pay off handsomely over the course of a lifetime—and, as we know, you'll be solving toughies deep, deep into your AARP years, because all this crossword fun has been beating back the armies of senile dementia.

My own invention for solving improvement is making a study of already-solved puzzles. When I was getting myself into fighting trim for the national championships, I discovered that a great way to increase my understanding of the way puzzles worked was simply not to solve them, but to cut out the clues for one day's puzzle, and then compare them with the answers published the next day. I pored over these clues and answers like they were religious texts, studying the forms of wordplay involved, the factual references used, and the unfamiliar words employed. With a month's worth of puzzles, all of them flawlessly answered by the newspaper itself, I could study hundreds and hundreds of clues and answers, gleaning a real understanding of crossword culture without ever putting pencil to paper. Yes, I know it sounds fanatical—but hey, it worked. And it continues to work: I've recommended this technique to many solvers who are completely stymied by my Saturday Stumpers, and they've reported after several weeks that they're able to make major inroads in the puzzle.

Once you've acquired the experience necessary to battle happily with even the most difficult crosswords, you'll likely begin to look at puzzles in a new way—as if you're seeing the grid the way a champion solver does. And that's markedly different from the way the average crossword fan looks at it.

An expert solver can tell from glancing across the room at an unsolved puzzle how difficult it is. If the puzzle grid is teeming with black squares (always in a symmetrical pattern—that's a longstanding crossword convention), then it has been pegged toward the casual solver. The black squares mean that there will be plenty of short words, which invariably means the solutions will be relatively simple. If, on the other hand, the grid is almost devoid of black squares, it's necessarily going to have many long answer words—words that are almost certainly going to be harder to guess than the shorter ones, but that are also going to require much more work to build from crossing words if you're not sure what they are. In the crossword business, these difficult puzzles with big patches of white and few black squares are called wide-open, or more informally, "chunky."

Now, chunkiness might be intimidating on first glance, but there are a couple of key traits in these difficult puzzles that any expert solver knows. The first is that when you look at the top of a chunky puzzle, the first three rows are likely to have almost no black-square interruptions—they're just a bunch of white squares stacked on top of each other, like cargo containers at the Port of Newark. That can be daunting, until you consider that the words in the top Across row also have to provide the first letters of all the words coming Down. The majority of words in the English language begin with consonants, so it's a good bet that these top-row words are going to contain a high concentration of consonants that will be the starter letters for the Down solutions. That means words with consonant clusters like the STR and GHT in STRAIGHT will be much more useful to a constructor than, say, the relatively vowel-heavy AU REVOIR. Constructors are always on the lookout for ways to cram consonants into the top row. My favorite inspiration: the clue "Big name in pies," which required the answer MRS SMITHS. Nine letters, only one vowel! That top-row answer was . . . top notch.

The unsolved bottom row of a chunky puzzle also gives away some of its secrets to the expert solver. The stacked white boxes at the bottom of the puzzle look just as indecipherable as the ones at the top, but consider: The bottom row going Across consists entirely of letters at the end of Down answers. The four most common letters that end words in the English language are E, R, S, and D. The letter E, of course, is a workhorse that ends verbs, nouns, adjectives—occurring in two-thirds of English words, including the word "English." E is for everything. (Let's pause here for a moment to honor the late writer Ernest Vincent Wright, who in 1939 produced the novel *Gadsby*, subtitled: "A Story of Over 50,000 Words Without Using the Letter 'E'." It's precisely what it sounds like. To avoid temptation, Wright tied down the "E" on his typewriter when he was writing lines like this one, from the first chapter in his E-less saga about the mythical town of Branton Hills: " . . . man didn't start his brain working. No. All that an adult can claim is a continuation, or an amplification of thoughts, dormant in his youth." Eerie, no?) The letter R provides good service, too, attaching to many verbs and making them nouns (give/giver), S is admirably pluralistic, and D is a past master. This quartet of letters has a high occurrence rate in the last lines of crossword puzzles—that's why you'll often encounter Across answers in the last row that involve phrases such as SESAME SEED, REAL ESTATE, and SORE LOSER. If you're concerned that you might find yourself eyeing the bottom row of a difficult puzzle and can't quite remember what those bottom-row-intensive letters are, rearrange E, R, S, and D into a mnemonic: REDS. Baseball aficionados and Warren Beatty fans shouldn't have any trouble with that one.

I hope that you won't have nearly as much trouble with puzzles of even the highest difficulty if you've taken to heart and put into practice the advice I've offered here. Crossword puzzles represent a splendid American invention that has spread throughout the world since their arrival almost a century ago. They challenge the mind, sharpen the wits, provide a bit of education, tease your powers of reasoning, reward hard work, frustrate the inattentive, crack a few jokes, and, most important of all, are a reliable source of cerebral entertainment. They have remained popular because they have evolved over time, starting out as a dictionary exercise and slowly, beginning in the 1950s, becoming a mirror of their times. Crosswords have a way of making us appreciate all over again, if we needed reminding, what an extraordinary gift we have in the written word—regardless of whether words are strung together in sentences or penciled into a crossword-puzzle | G | R | I | |.

AFTERWORD

Are You Ready to Rumble (or Sail) with Crosswords?

Now that you've learned how to build your own mental-fitness program with crosswords, I invite you to apply your newly acquired knowledge to the crosswords I create and edit. My home newspaper, the Long Island, New York, daily *Newsday,* has a new puzzle of mine every day. The *Newsday* puzzles are available for free at my Web site, www.StanXwords.com. Many books of my crosswords are available at local bookstores or from online booksellers. These include volumes of brand-new puzzles in specific subject areas such as novels, golf, movies, and TV—not to mention my *Million Word Crossword Dictionary* and upcoming *Million Word Crossword Answer Book* (scheduled for early 2007). I hope you'll check them out the next time you're in your neighborhood bookstore.

If you find my methods helpful, or if you have any questions about them, please do let me know. Here's how to reach me:

Regular mail: P.O. Box 69, Massapequa Park, NY 11762 (Please include a self-addressed stamped envelope if you'd like a reply.)

E-mail: StanXwords@aol.com

For an even more personalized approach to honing your crossword skills, I invite you to sail with me on my annual Crossword-theme Cruise. Please see below for more details on that.

—Stan Newman

INDEX